11 LESSONS IN SELF-LEADERSHIP

Insights for Personal & Professional Success

Larry Holman

A Lessons in Leadership Book
Lexington, Kentucky

ELEVEN LESSONS IN SELF-LEADERSHIP. First Edition.
Copyright ©1995 by WYNCOM. All rights reserved. Printed in
the United States.

Cover design by Sheri Wood. Printing by The Keystone Printery.

Holman, Larry.
    Eleven lessons in self-leadership: insights for personal and
professional success / by Larry Holman — 1st ed.
    "A Lessons in Leadership Book."
    ISBN: 0-9648829-0-6

10 9 8 7 6 5 4 3 2 1

This book is lovingly dedicated to
Bunny Holman
my life mate in business and at home,
whose firm grasp of reality compensates
for the design flaws in my brain.

It is my sincere hope that anyone who reads the book
— including our sons, Dan, Jason, Matt and Sean —
will find it food for thought and a framework
within which they can develop
a personal leadership style.

CONTENTS

ACKNOWLEDGMENTS

Eleven Lessons in Self-Leadership represents the fulfillment of a dream for me: a book written not by an individual but by the collective intelligence of an organization. As such, the book is a culmination of several years of serious consideration on my part. It became tangible only through the distillation, extension and synthesis of my ideas by the employees of WYNCOM.

It would be impossible to thank everyone who in some way contributed to the completion of this book, but I will try. First, I am eternally grateful to my business partner and "better half," Bunny Holman, President of WYNCOM. Also, thanks to Rose Frazier Cord, Chief Operating Officer and Chief Financial Officer; Anna Jarvis, Vice President of Operations and Administration; and Jerry Miller, Chief Executive Officer.

Very special thanks are due the members of the WYNCOM "writers bloc" for their diligence and creativity. Keith Elkins, Robin Roth, Paul Sanders and

ACKNOWLEDGMENTS

Jeff Walter helped spearhead the project along with longtime consultant Ken Davis and assistance from John McGill and Tom Wallace. Jack Furlong of Transylvania University also contributed several key ideas. And the WYNCOM organization as a whole played a major role in providing examples of self-leadership and lending its enthusiasm and support for the project.

The fine authors and speakers who currently work with WYNCOM also deserve a pat on the back: Stephen Covey, Sam Deep, Michael Hammer, Tom Peters, Lyle Sussman and Denis Waitley. And, finally, many thanks to our longtime partner Wilbur Simpson and his staff at The Keystone Printery.

FOREWORD

One of the first things I discovered about Larry
Holman was that he's a basketball man. Though I've
never seen him play, I've heard that he's a rugged compet-
itor who goes after the ball with fierce determination.
That's the kind of player I always liked on my teams:
tough and hard-nosed, but fair, and filled with passion
and desire for the game. These attributes are also essential to effective self-leadership.

Larry's basketball days, like mine, are fond memories now. He still loves the game, of course, and occasionally he gets out on the court and shows that he hasn't
forgotten how to hit the boards. But these days, his
greatest successes are coming not through basketball but
through his company, WYNCOM, Inc. – a living,
breathing example of self-leadership.

Although Larry's title is chairman, his job description is more like coach. For the last several years, he has
been leading his team to victory after victory – creating
a solid game plan, then providing guidance and support

from the sidelines as his team executes the plan. He has great confidence in this team, and for good reason.

My championship basketball teams succeeded on the strength of conditioning, fundamentals and team spirit. I think these principles apply in any situation. In Larry's case, he has built a team of inspired, mentally tough employees who are conditioned to overcome adversity on their way to achieving their shared goals. They are well versed in the fundamentals of their jobs, which revolve largely around positive communications, customer service and problem solving. And they work fluidly together, putting individual egos aside in pursuit of what's best for the team.

Larry Holman and WYNCOM have achieved remarkable growth while providing value for customers throughout North America. Their main product is "Lessons in Leadership," a distinguished speaker series featuring the world's preeminent authorities on personal and professional success. What a lineup! Stephen Covey. Tom Peters. Denis Waitley. Michael Hammer. Sam Deep and Lyle Sussman. My good friend Jim Harrick, who led the 1994-95 UCLA Bruins to the NCAA men's basketball title. All of these people, like Larry Holman, are winning coaches.

This book is filled with the insights that Larry has learned as a coach of a successful team. His team performs in the arena of business rather than sports, but business and life in general have a lot in common with sports; you'll find that the winners share the same characteristics. Occasionally Larry uses a sports metaphor to describe some aspect of self-leadership, but don't let that bother you if you're not a sports fan. Other times, he might refer to a popular movie or use some other example to illustrate his point. He'll also draw upon the collective wisdom of his team, which has played a key role in conceptualizing and writing this book.

I am pleased to have been involved with the work of Larry Holman and WYNCOM because I believe in the work they're doing. Read and learn from their book on self-leadership. They're champions.

Coach John Wooden

PREFACE

"Failure is not an option."

This simple but powerful declaration, made by one of the leaders of Mission Control in the smash movie *Apollo 13*, seems particularly meaningful to anyone in business. It serves as an urgent call to self-leadership. In today's fast-changing, ultra-competitive, high-stakes global marketplace, leadership is a matter of life or death. In order to stay alive, and especially to thrive, every organization requires the concentrated and unified efforts of every member. We need total organizational accountability. And we need to ask some tough questions about ourselves and our organizations.

For example, has your company allowed one person to become a permanent employee who:

> *. . . puts immediate personal gratification ahead of commitment to the company?*

> *. . . allows family and personal life to suffer because of a lack of balance?*

. . . looks to management to "take care" of him or her?

. . . engages in malicious obedience or vicious compliance?

. . . hesitates to speak out and aggressively knock on management's door when convinced that the organization is on the wrong track?

. . . refuses to take seriously all the management "ravings" about global competition and other potential threats to the organization?

If these descriptions fit anybody in your organization, wake up and smell the cappuccino! You may be rapidly on your way to extinction. The "guilty" parties need to read this book — and so do you and the other members of your organization. Effective leadership, after all, is a two-way street paved with constant communication and course correction.

Now, more than ever, we desperately need a new breed of leaders to emerge at all levels of our organizations. We need people who, regardless of their job titles, are ready, willing and able to rise to the diverse challenges inherent in this chaotic environment. We need fluid, flexible, liquid leadership — flowing smoothly through the organization, adapting to changing situations.

Let me clarify what I mean when I say that failure is not an option. I'm *not* talking about the kind of failure that comes from taking chances and being innovative. I *am* talking about failure to adapt, failure to grow, failure to tolerate experimentation. The irony is that one of the surest ways to guarantee the ultimate failure of an organization is the refusal to accept the kind of failure that is essential to progress. We need leaders who realize the difference between these two types of failures.

We also need leaders who clearly *expect* success and will be satisfied with nothing less than the best — from themselves and from those who work with them. We need leaders who realize the incredible power that expectations have in helping create reality.

We need leaders who realize that success is never final, that today's winner is often tomorrow's dinosaur. We need leaders who avoid complacency by constantly seeking improvement, moving ever closer to fulfilling their potential.

We need leaders who persevere, who do not give up when adversity rears its ugly head, as it always manages to do. We need leaders who stand firm in their commitment to excellence, who put every ounce of

> The collective intelligence of WYNCOM wrote this book. As author, my role was that of a conduit, helping channel this vast intelligence.

their heart, soul, mind and spirit into the "cause," or the organization's reason for being. We need leaders who understand that, as I'm so fond of saying, you can accomplish absolutely anything you can imagine if you don't always have to take the credit.

We need leaders who help others become their best, and who can readily step in and pick up the slack on those occasions when their colleagues are at less than their best. It is inevitable that people will have deaths in the family, illnesses, emergencies and plain old "bad days." Even organizations have bad days. The best organizations, however, have people who can readily step in and pick up the slack when the going gets tough — because they fully understand what we mean when we say, "Failure is not an option."

LEADERSHIP AT ALL LEVELS

The issue of changing times is an essential one if we are to talk seriously about leadership — of ourselves and of others — in the mid-'90s and beyond. It has become more and more apparent in recent years that, as someone has astutely pointed out, many of today's problems are the direct result of yesterday's solutions. The rules have changed and continue to change. We all, as individuals and as organizations, are being challenged to stay abreast of changes while taking proactive steps to bring about positive change of our own.

Everywhere we look, lines are being drawn in the sand. Increasingly, we are being asked to define ourselves in terms of "us" versus "them." Much of the recent management literature has even fallen prey to this syndrome, and managers have been the primary victim. In a marketplace characterized by extensive reengineering, downsizing, streamlining, flattening and other attempts to create more productive organizations, "management bashing" has become the trendy thing to do. But the fact is that we need to move beyond adversarial relationships, which do nothing to strengthen the lines of communication that are so vital to any sustained success. We need to build upon the common ground, while finding ways to benefit from the differences. That's why leadership at all levels is so needed.

We've all read about what today's employees want. Meaningful work, flexible schedules, the chance to be part of a winning team, opportunities for growth in a socially and environmentally responsible organization. They still want fair compensation for their work, too, of course, but the bottom line is made of much more than money.

It's easy to dismiss all the talk about "empowerment," "shared vision," "organizational culture" and "balance" as just so much New Age feel-good pap or as buzzwords rendered meaningless through overuse and misuse. But these ideas, when actually implemented rather than just given lip service, can spell the difference between mediocrity and greatness.

Research has demonstrated that the empowering, participative style of leadership produces greater long-term results than the traditional, authoritarian chain of command. If you disbelieve the data, listen to what today's most successful leaders are saying.

Listen to Wayne Smith, a Lexington, Kentucky, banker whom I've known for years. I like what he says about organizational culture. "Unhappy people don't deliver good service to anyone," Wayne says. "We feel that we need to continue to create an atmosphere in this organization where our people want to come to work, give good service to our customers, show people that they really mean something to us, show each other that we mean something to each other."

I also particularly like what Tom Peters says about the ideal workplace in his book *The Pursuit of WOW!* "I think work and business can be creative and exciting," Peters writes. "A hoot. A growth experience. A journey of lifelong learning and constant surprise."

And why not?

Lifelong learning is one of the keys to not only being successful but also enjoying the process. (At WYNCOM, we like to say that our mission is to "have a little fun and make a little money." It actually runs deeper than that, but that's a heck of a start!) Lifelong learning is essential for individuals and for teams, which must learn and grow together. We all have something we can teach to, and learn from, one another. Self-leadership doesn't mean living in a vacuum; it means recognizing the importance of concepts like the ones that make up this book . . . and practicing them!

Eleven Lessons in Self-Leadership is an example of what can be accomplished through the practice of these concepts. I think it's accurate to say that the collective intelligence of WYNCOM wrote the book. As author, my role was that of a conduit, helping channel this vast intelligence. Without the employees of WYNCOM, this project would not have seen completion. I had the vision, the dream. They had the dedication, the desire and the skills to make that dream a reality.

The format of this book is an indication of the value that WYNCOM places in such concepts as shared leadership, teamwork, lifelong learning and diversity. Each chapter contains material generated by WYNCOM employees and associates — including, in some cases, readings reprinted from the monthly *Lessons in Leadership* publication. We've also listed numerous sources you might consult to expand upon the ideas of *Eleven Lessons in Self-Leadership*.

Most likely, you have experiences that could be educational to others, including me and my associates at WYNCOM. Who knows, they might end up in a future book! If you'd like to share your thoughts, please write to:

> Larry Holman
> "Lessons in Leadership"
> P.O. Box 21890
> Lexington, KY 40522-1890

In the meantime, it is my hope that the lessons in self-leadership that I have learned — and that I have included in this book — will be of help to you and your organization. Lead on!

Larry Holman

LEAD
BY
EXAMPLE

CHAPTER

A few years ago, members of my staff, which then numbered four or five, presented me with a plaque that said:

"Which way did they go? How many were there? How fast were they going? I must find them. I am their leader!"

I'm still not sure who laughed longer, them or me. We all recognized the truth in the statement. Now that WYNCOM – the organization my wife, Bunny, and I founded – employs more than 100 people and is continually growing, I have had to face up to the fact that it functions just fine without me. I have relinquished my position of CEO but still remain as Chairman. Though I'm still actively involved in the company, helping to guide its vision as we prepare for the 21st century, most day-to-day decisions are made without me.

This whole idea is frightening to a lot of leaders and managers. I'm still struggling with it myself. But I'm slowly learning to let go. And that's the way it has to be.

Teddy Roosevelt once said: "The best executive is the one who has sense enough to pick good men to do what he wants done, and self-restraint enough to keep from meddling with them while they do it." Let's change "good men" to "good people," and Roosevelt's quotation makes for a fine leadership philosophy.

We're striving to create and sustain an empowered organization. I won't say we're completely there, but we've made great progress, and we're continuing to work at it. Much of the progress we've made has been a result of lessons we've learned from other successful and insightful people. We've learned from people like Stephen Covey, Tom Peters and Denis Waitley, as well as from watching other successful organizations. Therefore we realize the importance of a positive example, which is what we're trying to be in everything we do.

All of the other chapters in this book are essentially outgrowths of this first chapter, for leading by example means being aware of, and practicing, the many attributes of self-leadership. Today, if we are to successfully lead by example, we must do more than stay attuned to the vast changes that continue to sweep the world. We must also find ways to create positive change that will benefit our own organizations and the world.

We must recognize the importance of knowledge and use it as the building block for our relationships within and among our diverse organizations. We must explore new ways to benefit from the diversity that surrounds us. We must find better means to get things done, achieving our goals and then setting ambitious but achievable new ones. We must improve our performance through cooperation, maximizing our potential by striving toward shared goals.

We must forget worry, or find ways to make it work for us, refusing to be paralyzed by the uncertainties of the times. We must think more effectively, drawing upon our amazing collective intelligence, which so often goes largely untapped. We must refine our work habits, working not harder but smarter. We must keep up with waves of information that continuously wash over us, but we must also fight information overload by filtering out the "noise" from what is actually important. We must maintain a healthy balance between our work lives and our personal lives. And we must use the power of the self-fulfilling prophecy, the success of which has been well documented but which still remains a "secret" in many quarters.

> "Not the cry, but the flight of the wild duck, leads the flock to fly and follow."
> — Chinese proverb

If we do these things, I believe, we will be doing a good job of leading by example. And we will create organizations that consistently perform "in the zone." If you've ever been a part of a championship team — whether academic, artistic, athletic, business or something else — then you surely understand what I'm talking about. When you're in the zone, you are in control of the game. In the zone, the whole of the team is greater than the sum of its parts, constant communication and teamwork are a reality, everyone's abilities blend together to create *magic*, productivity and enjoyment go hand in hand, and there is absolutely no limit on what can be accomplished. When we lead by example, we do what we can to help our

5

organizations to perform in that zone. And what a feeling it is!

HEROES IN ACTION

A recent article in *Parade* magazine featured comments from Americans on who their heroes are. Daniel Boorstin, noted historian and former U.S. Librarian of Congress, made some interesting comments about the difference between heroes and celebrities. "The hero is known for achievements, the celebrity for well-knownness," Boorstin said. "The hero reveals the possibilities of human nature; the celebrity reveals the possibilities of the press and the media. Celebrities are people who make news, but heroes are people who make history. Time makes heroes but dissolves celebrities."

As much as I love sports (and music, for that matter), it disheartens me to see how many of today's "heroes" have earned that status merely for their ability to dunk a basketball (or play a guitar). They have become heroes by meeting pretty shallow standards, it seems, and many of them fall short in the area of setting a positive example.

Charles Barkley, the talented and entertaining NBA star who has been called the "Round Mound of Rebound," has often received as much attention for his controversial exploits on and off the court as for his all-star-caliber performance. While many aspiring basketball stars idolize Barkley, he scoffs at the notion that he is a role model. In a television commercial for an athletic shoe, he flatly stated, "I am *not* a role model." But isn't he? The shoe company that signed Barkley to a lucrative endorsement contract knows that he *is* in fact a role model. All disclaimers aside, the message implicit in these commercials is: Charles Barkley wears these shoes, so maybe you should, too. I think a certain responsibility accompanies — or *should* accompany — that kind of power. (To Barkley's credit, during negotiations between the NBA players union and the owners, he criticized players who sought to break the union, warning them that no one player is bigger than the game.)

Admittedly, there are differences between the worlds of athletics and entertainment and the world of "traditional" business (although, as distinctions continue to be blurred, this may no longer be the case). A basketball player is not a CEO or even a middle manager. In my opinion, these latter people, who have been placed in positions of authority, have even greater responsibilities to the people they lead. And the people they lead also have great responsibilities to the rest of their organization. That is what we mean by self-leadership in a world where everyone must be a leader. During these times of often mind-numbing change, we need all the strong, committed, passionate leadership we can get.

Wouldn't it be great to build an organization of heroes — employees who serve as an example and an inspiration to others?

One such employee at WYNCOM was Dennis Deppisch, who remains a shining model of self-leadership for our employees to follow. His "Whatever It Takes" philosophy, unfailing integrity and passion for the job were unmatched. (His example is discussed in greater detail in Chapter 7.) Although Dennis, who died in June 1995, would probably be embarrassed to be called a hero, he definitely is one in my book.

In *Forging the Heroic Organization: A Daring Blueprint for Revitalizing American Business*, authors Emmett C. Murphy and Michael Snell describe an enlightened organization that sees the interrelationship of everything on earth. This "heroic" organization, as a result, takes a holistic approach in all its enterprises, empowering its own people as well as its partners, who include even competitors. "Authentic heroes," the authors write, "are ordinary people who accept extraordinary responsibility to meet extraordinary challenges."

> "A lot of leaders want to tell people what to do, but they don't provide the example. 'Do as I say, not as I do' doesn't cut it. Of course, I'm not about to show players how to run or pass or block or tackle by doing these things myself. My example is in things like my high standards of performance, my attention to detail, and — above all — how hard I work. In these respects, I never ask my players to do more than I am willing to do. My own preparation for every game has to be exemplary."
>
> — Don Shula

As leaders, we have a powerful responsibility to be worthy role models for our peers and for those we want to lead. At the same time, we should find positive role models for ourselves, striving to model ourselves after people we respect. Positive role models motivate us to be our very best. They don't have to be famous; they can be people who have meant something to us on a very personal level. Our role models can be parents, siblings, former teachers or coaches, bosses or co-workers.

Of course, there are also negative role models. These are people whose examples motivate us *not* to become like them. As we learn from our own mistakes, we can also learn from the bad examples of others. Meanwhile, it can be enlightening to put ourselves in the shoes of the people we lead. How would you like to work for yourself? As a customer, would you buy your company's products? How would you like to be married to yourself, or have yourself for a parent? In short, what sort of example are you setting for those you lead?

One excellent way to make effective use of role models is through "mentoring" programs. The concept of mentoring – or pairing employees with others who can counsel and teach them – is important to leading by example and helping create what has been called a learning organization.

Of course, leading by example is a two-way street in a world where everyone is increasingly expected to exhibit leadership skills. Whether you're a "boss" or a "subordinate," you don't have to be influenced by someone else's mood. In other words, if your boss is having a bad day that doesn't mean you have to have a bad day; and if someone who works for you is having a bad day, you don't have to let that negatively affect you.

And if you're having a bad day — as we all do from time to time — you don't have to let it show to the people you lead.

THE EXAMPLE OF THE GOLDEN RULE

One essential "rule of thumb" for leading by example is the Golden Rule, which advises us to treat others the way we would wish for them to treat us. This rule for living — which has equivalents in practically every culture in the world — is basically applied common sense. This time-tested guideline for balancing individual rights and responsibilities transcends any legal requirements that might vary from state to state or nation to nation.

I've always liked Stephen Covey's interpretation of the Golden Rule, which grants strong consideration to the diversity that characterizes any organization or any family. In *The Seven Habits of Highly Effective People*, he writes:

> The Golden Rule says to "Do unto others as you would have them do unto you." While on the surface that could mean to do for them what you would like to have done for you, I think the more essential meaning is to understand them deeply as individuals, the way you would want to be understood, and then to treat them in terms of that understanding. As one successful parent said about raising children,

"Treat them all the same by treating them differently."

If we are serious about leading by example, we will treat others with the same respect with which we expect them to treat us. We will treat others fairly and keep the commitments we make to them. From the perspective of self-leadership, we also will be honest with ourselves, and will keep the commitments we make to ourselves.

Leading by example means walking the talk, practicing what we preach. We must ask nothing of someone else that we wouldn't be willing to do ourselves. "Do as I say, not as I do," a favorite saying of some parents to their children, is a cop-out, a slogan of irresponsibility. We should never make excuses to the people we're leading. The buck stops here.

Whatever our leadership role in the workplace, in the home, or in some other arena, we must lead with our actions more than our words. If we fail to do this, we lose the trust and respect of those we presume to lead. Human nature is such that it loves to see a hypocrite fall. Consider the gleeful reactions that many people had to the downfall of televangelists Jim Bakker and Jimmy Swaggart. A common reaction was "What right do these hypocrites have to tell me how to live?"

> "The speed of the boss is the speed of the team."
> —Lee Iacocca

Unless we want to be branded as hypocrites, we must be conscious of our own actions and whether they are consistent with our words. The supervisor who warns his employees about taking company paper clips for personal use but pads his own expense account is a hypocrite.

WYNCOM recently launched a project we called Mission Impossible. The goal was to stuff 1 million envelopes in-house for a division of the company that specializes in direct-mail marketing services. There were a couple of reasons for launching this project: to generate some bottom-line savings and, more important, to get employees involved in something that was fun and that also illustrated the principles of teamwork and synergy.

Mission Impossible began at a time that was less than ideal for many employees, who were in the midst of other project deadlines (in the business we're in, there's *always* a deadline looming; yours is probably no different). How could I show, rather than simply tell, our employees that this was an important project that I strongly believed in? The only way I could think of was to roll up my sleeves, get in the trenches and stuff some envelopes myself.

Now, you might think that stuffing envelopes is somehow "beneath" a company chairman, but I disagree. I'm no better than the others throughout the organization whom I was asking to support this goal. When I spent 12 hours — from 7 o'clock on a Thursday evening to 7 o'clock on Friday morning — stuffing 1,155 envelopes, I was making tangible my commitment to the goal. That's something I couldn't have accomplished in a dozen impassioned rah-rah speeches to my associates in the company.

LEADING, LEARNING, INTERRELATEDNESS AND CHAOS

The principles of self-leadership are not management theory. It is possible to agree intellectually with the lessons in this book and still be ineffective as a leader. That's because, unless accompanied by action, these principles are meaningless.

President John F. Kennedy, in remarks prepared for delivery in Dallas on November 22, 1963, said, "Leadership and learning are indispensable to each other." And leadership, like learning, cannot be achieved passively. Leaders must walk the talk. Leaders must first become *involved* before they can possibly engage the imagination and involvement of others.

In order to effectively lead by example, we must know ourselves, as individuals and as organizations. Who are we? Why are we here? What is our purpose? What are we capable of doing? What areas do we need help in? How do we plan to go about accomplishing our goals and fulfilling our potential? We must be honest — sometimes painfully so — about strengths and weaknesses. We must make a commitment to ourselves and to our partners that, if we're not happy about our current situation, we will do what it takes to change it for the better. (And we must be aware of the "law of unanticipated consequences," which says that our actions often produce unexpected results.)

Today, more than ever, our lives are inextricably connected with the lives of many other people. We must learn to accept, and act upon the fact, that we all are interrelated and interdependent. As a result, each of us has a great responsibility to the others in our families, in our organizations, in our world.

Knowing ourselves also means acknowledging the fact that none of us knows it *all*. As Socrates said, "I know nothing except the fact of my ignorance." People who have mastered the skills of self-leadership are fully aware of how little they know compared with what *can* be known. They are eager to learn as much as they can, becoming "students who lead."

> "On what does our salvation depend? On leaders. But we must agree on what we mean by a leader. A leader is one who governs without doubt. The manager also governs — he arbitrates and administers — but the manager is not a leader.... A leader is one who needs us, needs us ardently. He ... solicits not only our effort in the task at hand but our constant invention, that which transforms us into creators. Because he needs our creations.... Almost anyone can give orders, can impose himself upon us from the height of a throne. But in what way do these posturings of a corporal have anything to do with authority? Authority entails creation."
>
> — Saint-Exupery, French aviator and writer, from biography by Stacy Schiff (quoted in *Fortune* magazine, July 10, 1995)

As we learn more about ourselves, we also learn more about those around us. We realize that every person has an inherent uniqueness and value, and that this diversity can only enrich our lives and our organizations. We are open-minded toward others' ideas and beliefs. We realize that every situation has many alternatives, and that there is often more than one answer. Knowing these things, we strive to walk with truth while remaining open to alternatives and better ways to fulfill our potential. And we strive to build our lives on truth, integrity and honesty. Our interdependence, combined with the chaos that marks today's world, presents a compelling reason for us to recognize our responsibility and set positive examples in the lives we lead.

In his 1987 book, *Chaos*, James Gleick wrote: "Tiny differences in input could quickly become overwhelming differences in output. . . . In weather, for example, this translates into what is only half-jokingly known as the Butterfly Effect – the notion that a butterfly stirring the air today in Peking can transform storm systems next month in New York." In other words, the ripple effect created by our actions can stretch on almost infinitely.

Chaos, of course, can be a good thing. As historian Henry Brooks Adams wrote in his influential 1907 autobiography, *The Education of Henry Adams*, "Chaos often breeds life, when order breeds habit." And my friend and colleague Tom Peters, in *Thriving on Chaos*, taught us how to create total customer responsiveness, pursue fast-paced innovation, achieve flexibility by empowering people, learn to love change and build systems for a world turned upside down.

HABITS FOR LEADING BY EXAMPLE

As a leader learning to give up power and empower others, I'd like to share just a few of the habits I've learned that any leader needs to use in an organization. In my experience, these habits — in addition to character traits such as integrity, honesty, fairness, commitment and spirit — are essential to leading by example.

Accessibility. Leaders need to keep in touch. They need to be available to make sure that organizational objectives are understood and shared. They need to keep the communication lines open with other levels of management to make sure the right messages are communicated throughout the organization. Above all, they need to be around to listen to their people.

Support. Leaders need to make it clear that employees will be given the support they need — financial, moral, directional and otherwise — to carry out their tasks.

Recognition. Leaders should recognize significant individual and team contributions to the organizational mission. Team recognition tends to be even more valuable because it rewards cooperation.

Empathy. The American Heritage College Dictionary defines empathy as "identification with and understanding of another's situation, feelings and motives." Leaders should not only understand their organizations but also create an atmosphere by which team members understand one another. One excellent way to promote this is by cross-training. Cross-training has multiple benefits. It makes employees more versatile and more able to fill in for one another in a pinch. It aids in communication across functional boundaries and adds to employees' respect for one another.

Shared responsibility. Leaders should give their people important jobs. Effective delegation also brings multiple benefits. It empowers individuals to strive for new heights, confident in themselves and in their leaders' confidence in them. It also can bring out previously untapped sources of innovation and ingenuity. Everybody benefits.

As you've no doubt recognized, leading by example is a combination of self-knowledge and outward focus. As leaders, we must know ourselves, project ourselves, involve ourselves, be open to others, mentor when needed, build consensus when possible and be decisive when needed. We must show respect, and we must earn respect by being respectful.

When we are able to consistently achieve these goals, we will be effective leaders — and our organizations will thrive.

WORDS FROM WYNCOM

"Leadership is simply getting the job done — whether being a self-leader and doing it yourself, or getting others to work with you." — *Arthur Light*

"Self-leadership has a lot to do with knowing yourself. You first have to know yourself, what you want and how you can contribute your skills and talents to the overall objectives of the organization you're working for. . . . It amazes me how mature the young people we have working here at WYNCOM are and how they seem to be very capable of being self-directed and motivated. They really can see the larger goals of the company. — *Bunny Holman*

"Leading by example means expecting no more of some-one else than you expect from yourself. Leaders 'set the stage' or 'show the way.' Individuals need clear direction, and this is accomplished by setting the example."
— *Marty Adcock*

"Leading try to help in any way they can. Individuals need clear direction, and this is accomplished by setting the example." — *Ted Barnes*

"To be willing to do anything that is asked no matter what, for the common goal of making this or any com-pany the most successful possible." — *Doug Richard*

"If you are a manager and you are trying to motivate your subordinates, don't just preach at them — jump in and get your hands dirty with them." — *Kelly Bixler*

"When someone leads they should model the achieved goal through their actions. If someone wants to achieve a certain goal with integrity and hard work, then the leader needs to model that for the workers." – *Kyle Bixler*

"What better way to have someone believe what you say than by showing them that *you* believe it, too!"
– *Debbie Taylor*

"Have a contagious attitude; people tend to mimic actions of role models, so if you have a good leadership ability, people will catch on." – *Terri Cecil*

"Doing every aspect of the job in such a way that, no matter what the outcome, I can be proud of it. Doing even the small tasks in this manner regardless of who may or may not see the work being done. Meeting my own standards and re-evaluating them frequently." – *Tyra Swilo*

"To me, 'lead by example' means the ability to roll up one's sleeves and work side-by-side with co-workers, regardless of one's position in the company, no matter what the task." – *Anna Lee Ginter*

"Trying to set a professional example in working with everyone. Empathic, non-judgmental listening."
– *Anna Jarvis*

"At one of our first Texas programs we had site problems – there were large columns all throughout the room – and we also had sound problems. Larry said we owned every person's problem or complaint and to take care of the customer's needs. In other words, if a problem is brought to your attention, you own it." – *Rick Lewis*

"My background includes experience in human resources and employee services. When I joined the company, there was no established procedure for hiring. I put together an application form specifically geared to our company, offered my services to anyone needing employees, to facilitate the hiring process." — *Elaine Rutherford*

"The phrase 'to lead by example' means to me to take responsibility and charge of whatever needs to be done. This is especially true in my own life. You cannot lead where you have not gone." — *Linda J. Rogers*

"Leadership at WYNCOM has at least two facets: continually developing alliances with others and teaching myself new levels of awareness, so as to make the most of the present and help prepare for the future." — *Maureen Baxter*

"I believe that being in a role as a leader is not determined by your title, it is determined by your attitude. I would like to be a leader by simply doing my best at each task, no matter how quaint it may seem." — *Scott Via*

"Recently I volunteered to help with the company picnic. I organized the games and activities for the day. I feel as though I was a good example to others by taking the initiative to help. The picnic was a success, and I feel a sense of accomplishment and satisfaction."
— *Melissa Fightmaster*

"Upon accepting a position with this organization, I dedicated myself to doing the best job I could, to make whatever area I was assigned to run effectively and efficiently. I feel I took on a leadership role the day I was hired." — *Dan Lesher*

The Communicating Leader

Balance your communication

by Kenneth W. Davis

"It's not *what* she said; it's *how* she said it." "His *actions* are so loud, I can't hear what he's *saying.*" "She talked a lot, but she didn't *say* anything."

Comments like these describe the most common kind of communication failure — the failure to balance the two functions of communication. To communicate effectively, leaders need to find this balance.

Ko and *Mei* Communication

The word *communication* comes from the Indo-European words *ko* and *mei* (pronounced "may"), meaning "together" and "change." Some communication takes place primarily for the *ko* function of building or maintaining relationships, of keeping a community *together.* For example, greetings exchanged with coworkers, like "Hello" or "How are you?" have almost exclusively a *ko* function.

Other communication takes place primarily for the *mei* function of changing something, of getting something done. For example, a faxed order for a pepperoni pizza (no anchovies) may have almost exclusively a *mei* function.

Of course, most acts of communication have *both* functions. When we speak or write, we usually want both to maintain a relationship *and* to get something done. If you ask a coworker, "Robin, if you don't mind, would you please bring the first-quarter sales figures to the meeting?" you are trying to get the sales figures, but you are also trying to keep on good terms with Robin.

Language experts have used a number of labels for what I call the *ko* and *mei* functions of communication: "social" and "practical"; "identity-focused" and "task-focused"; "relation-oriented" and "content-oriented"; "interactional" and "transactional." Deborah Tannen, in such books as *You Just Don't Understand,* refers to these functions as the "meta-message" and the "message" and argues that women and men sometimes value them differently.

Questions for Leaders

But effective leaders, whether men or women, need to balance the *ko* and *mei* functions in what they say and write. To check *your* balance, ask yourself these questions:

1. Is my communication more "relationship-oriented" or more "content-oriented"? That is, do I tend to emphasize the *ko* function of togetherness or the *mei* function of change, of action, of getting things done?

2. If I am a *ko* communicator, how can I become more confident, more assertive, more willing to ask for *change* in other people's actions or opinions?

3. If I am a *mei* communicator, how can I become more supportive, more sensitive, more willing to postpone immediate results for the sake of ongoing *relationships?*

For further reading . . .

Anthony, William P. *Managing Your Boss* (Amacom). "You have more power than you think," Anthony's book says. It goes on to provide specific advice on influencing those above you in an organization through understanding your roles, shaping expectations, managing yourself, communicating, modeling behavior, and being a problem solver.

Apps, Jerold W. *Leadership for the Emerging Age* (Jossey-Bass). This book, while centering on practices in adult and continuing education, is a useful guide for anyone who wants to become a new kind of leader.

Bennis, Warren. *On Becoming a Leader* (Addison Wesley). This study of 28 business leaders has justly become a classic for its focus on how effective leadership takes place in real organizations.

Clemens, John K., and Steve Albrecht. *The Timeless Leader* (Adams). This book, on leadership lessons from great writers and leaders of the past, includes a discussion of the admonition that "you've got to learn how to follow before you can begin to lead."

Cohen, Allan R., and David L. Bradford. *Influence Without Authority* (Wiley). Like Anthony's book (listed above), this book makes the point that leadership doesn't require a specific block on a line-and-block chart; instead, it can be exercised, largely by example, at all levels of an organization.

Covey, Stephen R. *Principle-Centered Leadership* (Summit). While the entire book deals with "leading by example," Chapter 1, "Characteristics of Principle-Centered Leaders," is a powerful, short statement of the self-leadership necessary for effective leadership of others.

Covey, Stephen R. *The Seven Habits of Highly Effective People* (Simon & Schuster). Throughout this book, Covey makes the important point that interpersonal leadership must begin with personal leadership.

Crosby, Philip B. *Leading: The Art of Becoming an Executive* (McGraw-Hill). This useful book makes the important point that being an executive is not "like being a manager, only more so." Instead, Crosby argues, it requires new skills and new perspectives.

Deep, Sam, and Lyle Sussman. *Yes, You Can!* (Seminars by Sam Deep). Chapter 5, "Motivate Others," contains valuable tips on such goals as "Gain respect as a leader," "Create an inspiring vision" and " Find out how followers see you."

Murphy, Emmett C., with Michael Snell. *Forging the Heroic Organization: A Daring Blueprint for Revitalizing American Business* (Prentice Hall). Based on the Sioux concept of the interrelationship of everything, this book defines the leadership roles of all stakeholders in a company.

Peters, Tom. *The Tom Peters Seminar: Crazy Times Call for Crazy Organizations* (Vintage). Chapter 4, "Beyond Loyalty: Learning to think like an Independent Contractor," makes a lively, powerful case for self-leadership.

Renesch, John, ed. *New Traditions in Business: Spirit and Leadership in the 21st Century* (Berrett-Koehler). This book collects 15 inspiring and practical articles on achieving greater congruity between one's work and one's inner values.

Shula, Don, and Ken Blanchard. *Everyone's a Coach* (Harper Business and Zondervan). Using the acronym "COACH," Shula and Blanchard argue persuasively for a leadership style that is "conviction-driven," is based on "overlearning," is "audible-ready," is grounded in "consistency," and is "honesty-based."

Sinetar, Marsha. *To Build the Life You Want, Create the Work You Love* (St. Martin's). This sequel to the best-selling *Do What*

You Love, the Money Will Follow focuses on entrepreneurship as a vehicle for self-leadership.

Waitley, Denis. *Empires of the Mind: Lessons to Lead and Succeed in a Knowledge-Based World* (Morrow). Chapter 1, "Self-Leadership and Change," includes, on page 6 and following, a good section on how leaders emerge from times and change. Chapter 2, "Self-Leadership and Responsibility," discusses, on page 31 and following, ways of becoming the "CEO" of your own life.

Waitley, Denis. *Timing Is Everything* (Nelson). Chapter 10, "The Season for Taking on the Identity of a Successful Farmer," applies the habits of good farming to cultivation of effective leadership.

Wheatley, Margaret J. *Leadership and the New Science: Learning about Organization from an Orderly Universe* (Berrett-Koehler). This powerful book demonstrates that "leading by example" is not just a management fad; it is built into the very structure of our world. Chapter 4, "The Participative Nature of the Universe," offers examples from quantum physics of the ways in which we change our reality by our participation in it.

Zoglio, Suzanne Willis. *The Participative Leader* (Irwin). This slim book, highly "participative" in its own format, is a good introduction to leadership through employee commitment, self-motivation, and empowerment.

TURN KNOWLEDGE INTO MONEY

CHAPTER

2

Ahomeowner was relieved that a repairman was able to fix his furnace in a matter of a few minutes on a cold winter day, but was surprised when he was handed a bill for $50.

"Fifty dollars?" the homeowner exclaimed. "All you did was tap the furnace one time with a hammer!"

"Let me itemize that for you," the repairman said. He made some notes on the bill and handed it back to the customer. It read:

Tapping furnace with hammer – $1

Knowing where to tap – $49

The point is that you should not value work simply by the amount of time or effort it appears to take in its final stage. In this case, the customer was paying for the repairman's knowledge, not the effort taken. Have you ever heard someone complain that the boss or business owner "doesn't do any of the work"? While every employee's contribution is valuable, many fail to recognize that the person who had an idea is usually the reason the work exists at all.

How can you be the person who comes up with valuable ideas?

Study your company. Know its mission, and know the problems it faces, whatever your position in the company. If you're an owner or manager, make sure employees have the information they need to help you solve problems. Open-book management, in which employees have complete access to financial information, may not be for you just yet. But you should be able to find a comfortable middle ground that will allow you to take advantage of the problem-solving skills of your employees. If you're an owner or manager, make sure the employees know what your concerns and goals are. Chances are, "mind reader" isn't on anybody's resume. But if you don't clearly share your plans and goals, you are expecting employees to read your mind before they can really contribute.

Of course, if you're an employee who *can* read minds, your value to the company will rise significantly! Short of that, however, the more you know about your company, its market and its competition, the more likely you are to be the person who comes up with valuable ideas.

HOW MUCH DO YOU KNOW?

"Larry Holman, I'd like you to meet . . ."

Obviously, that statement would end with another person's name. I didn't include the other name because the statement, as printed, is all that many of us hear anyway. We catch our own name (yep, that's me, we think confidently), and wait for the person speaking to finish so that we can shake hands with . . . uh — what's-his-name.

Many books and courses have addressed the subject of remembering names. In business, you're only getting started when you remember a prospective customer's name. How much do you know and remember about that person's business? You don't have to be an outside sales representative to face those situations. What if you want to "sell" an idea to your supervisor? Do you know enough about that person's work to know whether your idea is in line with his or her goals and duties?

> **"Wealth is the product of man's capacity to think."**
> **— Ayn Rand**

If you're thinking only of selling your product or service, you're thinking only of *your* need — not the customer's. That's about as productive as coming away from an introduction with only one name in mind — yours.

A poll of purchasing managers originally printed in *Better Repping*, a newsletter published by Jack Berman of Encino, California, and reprinted in *Sales Secrets from Your Customers* by Barry J. Farber, asked what buyers considered most helpful in a salesperson. The number one answer was knowledge.

Under "most objectionable," the buyers listed lack of preparation and lack of information. Salespeople — and others — lose money every day because they have not made enough of an effort to accumulate knowledge about the people and businesses they are supposed to serve.

Here are some additional tips for turning knowledge into money:

Read! Read trade magazines and industry newsletters, not just from your own field, but from those with whom you do business. With the additional information and a better understanding of the work of others, you'll increase your ability to solve their problems — and you'll have more satisfied customers, supervisors or subordinates. In other words, you'll more effectively serve the people you work with — automatically increasing your value to them. (If you really believe you don't have time to read, Chapter 4 and Chapter 8 offer help on how to find the time.)

Improve your language skills. Your choice of words leaves an indelible impression on others. A strong resume, a good appearance and a firm handshake are no match for bad grammar or a limited vocabulary. In *Empires of the Mind*, Denis Waitley calls vocabulary "the new sword" in a knowledge-based world. He writes:

"In some of his earliest tests, Johnson O'Connor found a distinct correlation between vocabulary and career success. O'Connor consultants now stress the continuing importance of vocabulary. 'The aptitudes point which direction a person should go,' concludes an

O'Connor Foundation research paper, '(and) the vocabulary level predicts how far a person will go in his or her career.' Another way to say this is that limited vocabulary and feeble ability to communicate keep many people with excellent abilities of other kinds from developing them."

Talk to those who have done what you're trying to do. Have you ever heard of anyone making an important decision based on the opinion of a neighbor, friend or co-worker who has little or no experience in that field?

"I'd really like to start my own business, but Jane at work says I'd be crazy to leave with just 22 years to go before retirement."

(Of course, Jane has been with the company for 35 years and is just three years from retirement. She's also bitter about not taking advantage of opportunities earlier in life. Why should she have any influence on your decision? Unfortunately, we very often "unload" our most private thoughts and plans on those who are least equipped to really help us.)

"I thought about investing in that business, but Joe next door said he heard about someone who lost money."

(Joe probably has a passbook savings account and thinks the stock market is for millionaire high-rollers. Now, it is possible that Jane and Joe may be entirely correct in their assessments; accidents do happen. However, it would be best to seek advice from someone who has experience or certified expertise.)

Give some consideration to your sources of information. Can the person from whom you're seeking advice really give you the information you need? It would be staggering (not to mention depressing) to think of the opportunities, financial and otherwise, that have been missed because someone relied on a Jane or Joe as a consultant.

Take advantage of free information. The public library offers more than you think. Look into it, and really learn how the library can be used. Newspapers, magazines and reference materials

"Those who enter to buy, support me. Those who come to flatter, please me. Those who complain, teach me how I may please others so that more will come. Those only hurt me who are displeased and do not complain. They refuse me permission to correct my errors and thus improve my service."
— Marshall Field

can be of great help as you research your own business and those of your customers.

Know your business. This may seem obvious, but many people think they "know their business" if they know their own job description. If that's all you know, how can you ever go beyond your present level? Find out all you can about how your company operates. Annual reports, newsletters and conversations with employees from different departments would be a good start. Then talk with customers! What do they think about your company, and in particular about the work done in your area? If you do all these things on a regular basis, you will quickly move far ahead of the "that's-not-in-my-job-description" crowd.

In *To Build the Life You Want, Create the Work You Love*, author Marsha Sinetar tells of a young hair stylist who wanted to build his business by serving more affluent customers. In order to feel comfortable around the well-to-do, and in order to make them feel comfortable around him, he refined himself, smoothing out the rough edges. He signed up for elocution lessons, found them well worth the time and money, and went about building an upscale image that would match the clientele he wanted.

Review goals — of others! What is your company CEO's primary goal for this year? What is your supervisor trying to accomplish? What is at the top of your best customer's list of priorities? If you're not certain, ask to meet with them so you can find out! You may already have information that will help your company solve its biggest problem. Again, most purchasers say their biggest problem in working with salespeople is a lack of knowledge on the part of the salesperson. That principle carries over into other areas of work, not just sales. If you go into a meeting with the sincere intention (and the necessary information) to help someone else solve a problem, that person is going to see you not as a drain on his or her time and money — but as a valuable resource.

> **"Few of us can stand prosperity. Another man's, I mean."**
> — Mark Twain

Sinetar also quotes a computer repairman who kept his job at a time when many other middle managers were being let go by their companies: "I've made it my business to improve myself each year, to diversify my skills, to give customers more than they expect whenever possible. Going the extra mile routinely is a discipline for me — I wake up early each morning and sit in my garden with my coffee, and reflect on how I can better serve my customers. No one tells young people about this self-training, but that's what it takes to succeed."

Turn money into money — with knowledge. I know that's not exactly the title of the chapter. But it's logical that turning knowledge into money will require a little knowledge of money. Financial planning has become more important than ever as more Americans rely on themselves for a stable financial future. I suggest a study of the basics of financial planning, so that when you meet with an expert, you'll be better able to understand the advice you receive. If this is new to you, start with financial advice columns in newspapers, which are generally written for non-experts. And as I mentioned earlier, the library can be an excellent place to begin your studies.

Before you make any decisions about investments, make sure you know how you feel about money. Many people can state their financial goals only one way: "I'd like to make a lot of money." Well, how much? A lot to me might not be a lot to you. A good rule of thumb is that the amount of money you need to make is the amount it takes to keep you from worrying about money.

For some people, that might be $25,000 a year. Others couldn't sleep at night if they made less than $500,000 a year. You may not consider yourself a person who is motivated by money, but that's a great reason to analyze your needs — and then you really can keep money worries out of your life. The questions to ask are:

> "The want ad section of the newspaper is what people are all about—not the front page. In the want ads, you see what people want, and what they want to get rid of. This gives me ideas.
> — Roger Von Oech,
> *A Whack on the Side of the Head*

How much money do I want and need to make?

Can I do that with my present skills and experience? (In other words, have I examined the goals of others and discovered how I can offer a product or service that will help them reach those goals — making me valuable to them?)

If my financial goals do not match up with my skills and experience at this time, which should I change — the financial goals or my skills and experience? You can take it from there — and you can bet (although that's not a sound financial planning idea) that some additional knowledge will be needed if you decide to stay with your original financial goal!

WORDS FROM WYNCOM

"While working on a project with tight time constraints, I realized we could be more efficient. After timing myself to prove that this method was taking longer, I suggested that we do the project the more efficient way because we had the inventory available." – *Maureen Baxter*

"A company is only as good as its people. I strive to learn something new everyday so that this knowledge is turned into money." – *Anna Chapman*

"Managing for profitability means: 1. Make sure everything is done right the first time. 2. Order only enough material to accomplish your task. 3. Cut out unnecessary expenses. 4. Do everything you can to maintain your existing client base, because it's approximately four times as expensive to establish a new customer as it is to maintain an existing customer." – *Carl Swieterman*

"Know your options within the company! Again, knowledge of areas other than the one you work in helps the entire organization. We are our own best friends."
– *Tyra Swilo*

"Managing for profitability means to use the resources that one has and to use them in such a way that one can gain the maximum productivity potential from them, all the while spending as little as possible to achieve the goal of making a profit." – *Kyle Bixler*

"Managing for profitability means efficiency. Increasing efficiency increases profits." – *Carolyn Coffey*

"Managing for profitability means getting the most for your buck. As an empowered staff, we all have a responsibility to manage any costs we have control over. In the registration area, we have the opportunity to turn canceled registration dollars into product sales. As travelers, we often have choices to make regarding food or transportation. Using the various ideas, knowledge and experience of our diverse staff for improved and more efficient ways of doing things is a great cost-saver." – *Marty Adcock*

"Managing for profitability means trying to do the best possible job at the lowest cost without sacrificing the quality of your customer service. This maximizes the profitability of our programs, and Larry likes it, too!"
– *Russ Lampe*

"Managing for profitability means looking at the long-term effects of expenses and financial risks. For example, as a meeting professional I follow the philosophy that small leaks can sink a mighty ship, meaning it might be only 50 cents a plate you're saving; however, it is 50 cents times 1,000 meals times 120 meetings. In short, over a course of a year you can save $60,000 by just saving 50 cents per meal. I know that watching 50 cents per plate is more important than saving $4.00 a gallon on coffee, because we order fewer gallons of coffee than meals. This is a very simple concept, but it can make a big difference over the long term." – *Laurie Shipp*

"Managing for profitability means tackling a job assignment using the least amount of resources possible to obtain the highest standard of completion."
– *Dan Lesher*

"The phrase 'managing for profitability' means using all assets for maximum profit. This may be correct placement of people into positions where they can use their talents well, getting every ounce of profit out of an idea, or cross-pollinating an idea so it is beneficial in several areas of an organization. Every contact I make for Lessons in Leadership, I look for something else I can tell, sell or give as an extra service. I believe that excellent service will promote long-term profitability for us and will happily bind our clients to us. When I send out materials in marketing, I always remember to cross-pollinate by sending out information on another service or product we provide." – *Linda J. Rogers*

PROFILE: WAYNE L. SMITH

Leadership tips you can *bank* on

by Jeff Walter

Wayne L. Smith likes to joke about how he became president of Central Bank & Trust Co. "I stuck around and won by default," he says.

In all seriousness, his path to the top, like most success, was anything but smooth. After graduating from high school, Smith served in the Coast Guard; got married and started a family; worked as a collector for a finance company; went to college three nights a week for nine years; held positions with three banks, including senior vice president and senior lending officer for one that failed five months after he came aboard; and was for three months an unemployed father of four. In May 1975 he accepted a position as executive vice president at Central Bank in Lexington, Kentucky. A little more than a year and a half later, after the death of the founding president and a fast exit by two other presidents, Smith was named president.

These days, Central Bank is a hot commodity, with deposits on the rise while other local banks' deposits are declining. In a region that has been marked by bank merger upon bank merger, Central Bank proudly proclaims itself as "Lexington's last great independent bank."

Smith, who is now the bank's chairman and CEO, credits experience rather than schooling for his business philosophy, which he acknowledges is not unique. But at the same time, it's not as common as it should be. "I was with three other banks before coming here, and I think you can learn a lot from seeing things done the wrong way. Coming up through the ranks, I would see the CEO or my boss make a decision, and I'd say to myself, 'I wish I'd been able to make that decision; I wouldn't have made it that way.' "

Now that he's making the decisions, he hopes to help others do the right thing. When he retires, he'd like to teach at a state university, where students can supplement their academic learning with some lessons learned the hard way, in the real business world.

Here are some of the lessons he'd like to share:

Put the employee first: "We have got three important groups of people in our bank: customers, shareholders and employees. But we put it in a different perspective. If you look at our annual report, you don't see a 'letter to the shareholders.' It says: 'to our shareholders, customers and friends.' Shareholders are very important to our bank, especially when nearly 10 percent of our stock is owned by our employees.

"We don't make the customer or the shareholder first. The employee is first. Unhappy people don't deliver good service to anyone. We feel that we need to continue to create an atmosphere in this organization where our people want to come in to work, give good service to our customers, show people that they really mean something to us, show each other that we mean something to each other. Everybody's providing service to somebody.

"You can have a good bottom line and still treat people decent. As a matter of fact, if you treat 'em decent, you'll have a better bottom line in the long run. We have employees who are stockholders in this bank. It's important to them that this bank does well. It's important to them that this bank gives good customer service. It's important to them that we grow. If you stick around this bank for 15 years — let's say, as a teller — in March after you leave, you're going to receive about 150 shares of Central Bancshares stock from our ESOP (employee stock ownership plan) that didn't cost you a thing. And today the market price is $103 a share.

"If we do all those things, and do them right, then our customers, our second important group, are going to tell their relatives, their friends, their neighbors that Central Bank is the place to go. There are 10 banks in this town. The only niche we've got is to out-perform them and give better service. If we do that, then the bank grows. If the bank grows and invests its money properly and doesn't make a lot of bad loans, then the shareholders get a dividend every quarter.

"I will soon celebrate my 80th quarter in this bank. And we've paid a dividend 78 quarters."

Value your front-line people: "Teller should be the best-paying job in a bank, but it's not. We hire these young people who graduate from college with marketing degrees and can't get a job. Three months later they get a marketing job and leave the bank. But when we hire a group of new tellers, we put them through three weeks of classroom training with our training director before they hit a teller window. Then they go out to a branch and work for three weeks with another trainer, a teller we pay extra to train. Then we have a graduation breakfast, and I meet with them. I have a chance to talk to them about service.

"I let them know that 86 percent of our customers deal only with the teller, so the teller has to do the right thing. We can't be spending $300,000 or $400,000 each year on advertising and have our contact people running customers out the back door because we gave them poor service."

Be clear about your philosophy: "The biggest problem for a CEO is making sure that the leadership and management are all under the same philosophy. I always end my graduation-breakfast talk by saying to the new tellers: 'You've sat here for an hour and we've talked about management style and how I want this bank run. Now, when you get back to your branch this afternoon, you might see something that doesn't click with what I've just said to you. There might be a manager out there who's not going to manage the way Smith said he should. He might not treat people the way I want them treated. Just remember this: He's wrong, and I'm right. Don't get confused. And if you see too much of it, then you need to let somebody know, and as a matter of fact you need to call me and let me know.' "

Use common sense: "You don't need a graduate degree to be able to manage people. Most decisions that I make every day — that most of us make — are common-sense decisions. If you're going to be a leader, if you're going to manage people, just make sure you treat everybody exactly the way you want to be treated. And keep in mind that it's difficult to manage people only if you're having difficulty managing your own life."

Keep the doors open: "The leadership is very open in this organization. We don't close doors. My door hasn't been closed in 19 years. I don't believe in closed doors. When I walk through this bank and see a door closed, I normally walk in and see what's going on."

Answer your own phone: "There's no voice mail in this bank, except when we close the operator station at 5 o'clock and a recording comes on. We all have our own phone numbers. If I'm sitting here by myself and my phone rings, I answer it. We have no secretaries. We have associates to help us with our work. They aren't hired to make coffee or answer phones.

"When you answer your own phone, it amazes the caller sometimes. And you can really learn what's going on in your own company. When I answer this phone at 8:30 in the morning and a man yells, 'Are you chairman of that . . . bank?' well, I know he doesn't want to talk about the basketball team. He wants to tell me that the drive-in windows at our Southland branch are lined up to the street, and I need to get out there and do something about it.

"We have a newspaper ad that we're running against this Liberty/Bank One merger. It talks about our Bill of Rights, which says you have the right to get good service, and you have the right to get your money back after 90 days if you don't like your service. The headline says: 'For all of you who hold Liberty dear, Central Bank has a Bill of Rights.' And then it says, 'If you don't get it, don't hesitate to call me personally on my direct line. The number is 253-6200.' I signed it, and that's my own phone number. The ad doesn't say call the bank or customer service; it says call me! When we ran a similar ad a couple of years ago, I'd answer the phone and people would say, 'Mr. Smith, we just wanted to make sure that was really your phone number.' "

Build long-term, personal relationships: "People bank with the banker and not the bank. That's the key to this whole thing. If Luther Deaton, our president, left and went to another bank in town, he'd take a lot of business with him. He brought the business in here, and those people are going to go with him. The key is trying to keep your people. We have pretty good tenure among our managers, our assistant managers and our personal bankers — those people who open your accounts."

Recognize good customer service: "We've got a program called Expect the Best that I put into effect five years ago. It's a plaque that says, 'For enhancing service extended to our customers.' For the first few years I was here, I was getting five complaints on our service to every one compliment. It was tough. I was hiring customer service reps just to handle complaints. Then about 10 years ago we got it turned around. Today we get 40 to 50 compliments to every one complaint. The first time you as an employee get a compliment, you get a plaque with an apple, and I deliver it to you.

"In five years we have over 3,000 of these apples on plaques. Many of them don't come from customers. Guess who they come from? Fellow employees who say, 'I needed this research done for my customer, and Sally stayed until 6 o'clock last night to put it together for me, and I think she deserves an apple.' Those are the kinds of things that are meaningful to people."

Keep your people busy . . . and employed: "In my 20 years here, this bank has never downsized by laying off anybody. I've had to recommend that a few leave. We've gone from 309 employees in 1986 to 252 in 1994, but not from laying anybody off. By attrition. Of course, when we outsourced our data processing business, that eliminated a lot of jobs. But we decided seven or eight years ago that, when somebody leaves, we need to identify whether we really need to fill that position. In some cases, we probably had too many people doing that job anyway. If the remaining people can handle it, we'll let them do it — and add something extra to their base salary.

"My philosophy is: People never quit their jobs because they're too busy. They quit because they don't have enough to do. They're bored."

Promote from within: "What turns me on is seeing young people come up. I love to move somebody from this job to this job, and see about six people come up with him or her. We try to fill positions from within; we don't go out on the street and hire people. I've done it a couple or three times, and it amazes me. I have to make sure that the chemistry's right, that people can fit in this work environment, because it's different. When you move somebody into a position, there's a risk. And I would rather take a risk with my own people. If we just give them the opportunity . . .

"I wasn't ready in 1976 when they named me president! But do you think I told anybody? You've got to give people a chance and then support them. Move them in. Help them get ready. That's the fun you get out of this."

Give back to the community: "We put something back into this community. Our people volunteer hundreds and hundreds of hours back into this town for everything. And we put back a large amount of our bottom-line earnings in the form of contributions, donations, sponsorships and all those things. That's important."

The Communicating Leader

The long and short of it

by Kenneth W. Davis

American business is often criticized for its "short-termism." Fairly or unfairly, U.S. executives, boards of directors and shareholders are charged with obsessive attention to the current quarter's profits, at the expense of longer-term growth. We all seem to be victims of a "what have you done for me lately?" syndrome.

Whether or not that's a fair rap, it's certainly true of our communication. In the talking and writing we do, most of us tend to focus on immediate, *short-term* effects rather than *long-term* effects. We tend to speak or write for today or tomorrow, not for next year, next decade or next century.

To be more effective leaders, we need to change that. We need to master long-term as well as short-term communication.

Communication in Systems

To understand the difference between long-term and short-term communication, let's consider how communication functions in living systems. All living systems, from single cells to the global ecosystem, share certain characteristics. Some of these characteristics have to do with how systems process information — how they communicate. In fact, communication is what makes a system a system, not just a random collection of parts.

In her book *Leadership and the New Science*, Margaret J. Wheatley discusses this fact. "In a constantly evolving, dynamic universe," she writes, "information is the fundamental ingredient, the key source of structuration — the process of creating structure. Something we cannot see, touch, or get our hands around is out there, organizing life. Information is managing us."

She continues: "For a system to remain alive, for the universe to move onward, information must be continually generated. If there is nothing new, or if the information that exists merely confirms what is, then the result will be death. Isolated systems wind down and decay, victims of the laws of entropy. The fuel of life is new information — novelty — ordered into new structures. We need to have information coursing through our systems, disturbing the peace, imbuing everything it touches with new life."

Cells and Organizations

Consider the cell. In a cell, some information is long-term, stored in the cell's DNA. As the cell reproduces, this information is communicated from generation to generation. The "stuff" that makes up the cell may change, but this long-term information remains relatively constant.

By contrast, some information in a cell is short-term, in the form of electrical or chemical "messages" sent within the cell and between the cell and its environment. For example, such a message might carry information about temperature changes.

In an organization, too, some information is long-term, relatively permanent, allowing the organization to preserve its identity even as its members come and go. By contrast, some information in an organization is short-term, relatively temporary, allowing the organization to stay responsive and alive.

Questions for Leaders

To check your mastery of both short-term and long-term communication in *your* organization, ask yourself these questions:

1. Is my communication more short-term or long-term in its focus? That is, do I tend to communicate in order to build immediate relationships and get immediate results, or do I tend to ignore immediate goals and take a longer view?

2. If I am a short-term communicator, how can I get a longer-term perspective? How can I start thinking more in terms of goal statements, mission statements, vision statements and value statements?

3. If I am a long-term communicator, how can I focus more closely on the immediate relationships and short-term results that I need in order to realize my long-term goals and visions?

For further reading . . .

Barker, Joel Arthur. *Future Edge: Discovering the New Paradigms of Success* (Morrow). Barker, the "paradigm man," shows that by recognizing and defining the very lenses through which we see the world, we can predict, manage, effect and profit from change.

Brown, Barbara B. *Supermind: The Ultimate Energy* (Harper and Row). This book argues that beyond the brain, even beyond the conscious mind, lies a "supermentality" that "possesses prodigious abilities for reason, judgment, and altruism."

Buckholtz. Thomas J. *Information Proficiency: Your Key to the Information Age* (Van Nostrand Reinhold). This thorough, common-sense guide to managing information suggests detailed, specific strategies for profiting from new levels of information availability.

Campbell, Susan M. *From Chaos to Confidence: Survival Strategies for the New Workplace* (Simon & Schuster). In this book, Campbell argues that businesspeople, collectively and individually, must move from a "security/control" attitude to a "learning/discovery" attitude. She presents "six strategic meta-skills" for developing, and profiting from, this attitude.

Davidow, William H., and Michael S. Malone. *The Virtual Corporation: Structuring and Revitalizing the Corporation for the 21st Century* (Harper Business). Based on global case studies, this book defines the new structures necessary for companies whose most important asset is not materials but information.

Davis, Stanley M. *Future Perfect* (Addison Wesley). This book, perhaps more than any other, conceptualizes specific ways that knowledge can be turned into profits, through approaches that Davis gives titles such as "any time," "any place," "no-matter" and "mass customizing."

Deep, Sam, and Lyle Sussman. *Yes, You Can!* (Seminars by Sam Deep). The list on page 45, headed "Expand your Knowledge," is a good, brief set of tools.

Handy, Charles. *The Age of Paradox* (Harvard Business School Press). No one has more clearly detailed the implications of knowledge-based organizations than Charles Handy, perhaps Europe's leading business guru. Chapter 10, "The Intelligence Investment," in particular, explores the challenges and opportunities of the new information economy.

Naisbitt, John. *Global Paradox: The Bigger the World Economy, the More Powerful Its Smallest Players* (Morrow). Of special interest to the entrepreneur — but with value to all businesspeople — this book makes the dramatic case that the new global information economy makes it possible for even the smallest organizations to compete and win.

Naisbitt, John. *Megatrends: Ten New Directions Transforming Our Lives* (Warner). Though published in 1982, this classic book still provides one of the clearest available pictures of the transformation from industrial society to information society.

Naisbitt, John, and Patricia Aburdene. *Re-inventing the Corporation: Transforming Your Job and Your Company for the New Information Society* (Warner). A sequel to *Megatrends,* this book focuses on the organizational implications of the shift from an industrial to an information age.

Peters, Tom. *The Tom Peters Seminar: Crazy Times Call for Crazy Organizations* (Vintage). The section "Leveraging Knowledge," beginning on page 161, is an excellent introduction to turning knowledge into money.

Senge, Peter M. *The Fifth Discipline: The Art and Practice of the Learning Organization* (Doubleday). This powerful book, which popularized the term "learning organization," is an exciting, practical survey of what Senge calls the "core disciplines" of business — personal mastery, mental models, shared vision and team learning — and the fifth discipline, systems thinking, that unites them and turns them to business advantage.

Toffler, Alvin. *Power Shift: Knowledge, Wealth, and Violence at the Edge of the 21st Century* (Bantam). With a global scope, this book by the author of *Future Shock* examines the relationships between knowledge and wealth, in business, in politics, in society as a whole.

Waitley, Denis. *Empires of the Mind: Lessons to Lead and Succeed in a Knowledge-Based World* (Morrow). Pages 9 through 12, and following, effectively make the case that now, as never before, "knowledge is power."

BENEFIT FROM DIVERSITY

CHAPTER

I'm a middle-age white male born in Louisville, Kentucky, a city whose citizens to this day argue whether they are part of the South or the North. To the outsider, it's probably more accurate to describe them as both.

As a child I defined my boundaries as did most of my generation: family, friends, neighborhood. My first remembered contacts were with my mother's large family, aunts who spoiled me and uncles and older cousins who taught me to play sports — particularly my first love, basketball. Later, when I expanded my boundaries beyond family, it meant playing with kids in the neighborhood with the same backgrounds as mine, and attending schools with children who looked the same as I did and had basically the same things in common. Feeling happy and safe within my "comfort zone" of family and social relationships of people who were like me, I, like most in my peer group, spent my childhood forming my personal identity — unique certainly, but carefully enclosed within the commonalities of my own group.

While the script of my life is different from yours, essentially the plot is the same. Contemporary psychologists tell us that when we are born, it is our natural egocentrism that allows us to survive. As babies, we are concerned only with having our basic needs met. When we get older, we gradually expand our interests to include first the larger world of our family of origin, then friends and finally the community at large. It is within those groups that we create close ties, usually lasting as we mature into adulthood. While the specific individuals may change, we continue to associate with people who the ego tells us are like ourselves, based upon our early experiences. To a large degree, this is how we form our sense of who we are.

In this process, we meet people we feel are different from us, and make choices on how to react within the situation. In the broadest sense, when we make such choices, we have our first opportunity to encounter diversity and to discern its value.

My own encounters with the value of diversity seemed to be formulated around what I spent most of my childhood doing: playing basketball. Whether on the playground, at junior high school or starting as center for my high school team, there was only one

> "If we all pulled in one direction, the world would keel over."
> —Yiddish proverb

goal for everyone on the team: *Win the game.* While team members may or may not have had other interests, peer groups, backgrounds, race or socioeconomic class in common, when it came to performance on the court, working together to "go for the winning shot" was all that mattered.

While my basketball career is long-gone, understanding the process of our early encounters with others gives us the opportunity to decipher the origins of our attitudes and discern how we choose to react to new situations and people in our lives. With this understanding of our own backgrounds, we can then examine how we look at diversity in our present lives and careers.

DEFINING DIVERSITY

In recent years, diversity has been cast as a sociopolitical component of social planning or as a business performance issue. Both can apply. But I believe that the more broadly diversity is defined, the more effectively the definition can be used.

In a general context, diversity came under its current public scrutiny due to changes in the American workforce that started in the 1980s and continue today. The workforce is now made up of larger and larger percentages of Hispanic, African-American and Asian-American populations, as those groups have grown within the American population. In addition, immigrants are coming to the United States from all over the world, fleeing economic and political situations. Paralleling this change has been the movement of women into the workforce in record numbers. Add a new awareness of minority groups such as the disabled, who had been largely barred from the workforce, and a broad definition of diversity emerges.

Beyond this largely sociological definition, diversity can be considered more specifically from the organization's point of view. In this context, it includes race, age, gender, ethnic background, religion, physical ability, body size, sexual orientation, education and economic class. It also encompasses thinking styles, personality types, job function, professional specialities and life experience differences.

Organizational diversity can be seen in the way each individual views the company. For example, at WYNCOM, 71-year-old Arthur Light, who has been with the company since its inception, views the company very differently from database administration worker Scott Via, 24, who has been on the job less than a year. Effie Burge in Accounting sees the

> "If we cannot end our differences, at least we can help make the world safe for diversity."
> — John F. Kennedy
> address at American University, Washington, D. C.
> June 10, 1963

organization differently from Rick Lewis in Distributing. On a managerial level, Rose Frazier Cord, Chief Operating Officer and Chief Financial Officer, sees it differently from Anna Jarvis, Vice President of Operations and Administration. Add to this diversity of organizational function and occupation the versions of ethnic, gender and the other categories listed previously, and the variations of diversity broaden even more.

Defining diversity in this broad scope ultimately distills into a basic premise: Each person is a unique individual who can bring a unique perspective and creative contribution to the task at hand. While ethnic and cultural differences may be important, they should not be focused on exclusively. The validity of diversity is ultimately found by understanding that it encompasses all differences between individuals, an effect that strengthens and empowers individuals, organizations and the community at large.

VALUING DIVERSITY

Enthusiasm for the value of diversity was boosted with the publication of the 1987 Hudson Institute report *Workforce 2000: Work and Workers for the 21st Century,* which revealed dramatic changes in the American labor force. According to the report, by the year 2000, people of color, immigrants and women will constitute 85 percent of people entering the workforce, with white men born in this country comprising only 15 percent. While awareness of these changing demographics made diversity a new watchword, changing global economies and American desires to do business in foreign countries put it into bold type.

The value for diversity in this context is clear: Businesses, employees and clients are changing more rapidly than ever before. This necessity has created a need for awareness of the value of diversity and, in particular the opportunities that it can present in the marketplace. Valuing differences in a business makes a strong case when it has to do with developing new products or markets.

On an organizational level, diversity is valued for the ability to accomplish the task at hand. Bringing together different viewpoints — cultural, gender, ethnic and others — can allow for a creativity that might otherwise not be put in motion. The greater the diversity of the organization, the greater the potential for such creative power, if those differences can be channeled to achieve common goals, such as the success of products.

Diversity for the organization can mean developing relationships with co-workers who have different views from your own. The strength of such diversity is that it points to the fact that there are often real differences among the values of different groups. My own experience in founding a company with my wife made it clear to me that women often do look at situations differently from men. And more important, these differences matter. I readily and frequently acknowledge that WYNCOM would not have been created had it not been for Bunny. She brings not only a female perspective and a different method of decision making, but also, with her background in working with Japanese cultural programs, insight into approaching problems differently.

WYNCOM initially had the opposite male-female ratio of many American companies: Women were overwhelmingly in the majority in every area. The company had received recognition from a women's professional group for developing positions for women. As more men were brought into the company, new ways of communicating opened up. The differences reflected varying approaches and styles to the way these two groups approached everything from problem solving to general life outlook.

The reasons for valuing diversity continue to expand. While historically these reasons may have grown out of the women's rights and civil rights movements, today's emphasis suggests a focus that has shifted beyond fairness, morality and legal issues. Diversity can create new innovation and learning in business organizations, which may ultimately result in a more human and stimulating work environment for all.

> "Ask for dissenting views. Tell people that you want your assumptions challenged. 'Your job is to keep me out of trouble by preventing me from making foolish mistakes. I want each of you to take a few minutes right now to write down five potential disadvantages of my plan. Only when each of you is done will we proceed.'"
> — Sam Deep and Lyle Sussman,
> *What to Say to Get What You Want*

MANAGING DIVERSITY

Given that diversity has value, it is an asset of the organization — one that must be managed, just as any asset would be. The differences that each individual brings to the organization will inevitably cause conflict if not acknowledged, confronted, and resolved. Conflict can be creative, if positive results can be extracted from it. It can also generate more conflict, if not dealt with effectively.

Conflict is first of all generated internally — and management of conflict must also begin internally. In one of my early career positions, I went to work for a company run by three women. For the first time, I found myself a minority in management. Some of my male friends made fun of me because I worked for three women, and in fact, some of my female acquaintances questioned working for a woman. Keep in mind that these were the days when there were "serious" management books on subjects like "how to get along with women in the workplace."

> "A company in which anyone is afraid to speak up, to differ, to be daring and original, is closing the coffin door on itself."
> — Leo Burnett, *100 Leo's*

The woman who was my direct supervisor, Betsy Ross, confronted the potential conflict directly and thoroughly. Recognizing my internal conflict, she encouraged me to openly and appropriately examine and discuss my viewpoints and attitudes. She initiated conversations comparing our different styles and approaches to problem solving. (She was certainly more organized than I was!) She also did not hesitate to compliment my work or offer suggestions when she felt another approach would be helpful. Finally, she insisted that I was given credit for any project I worked on, making sure that I felt I was part of the team.

In managing my own company for diversity, I have often reflected on the experience that I was afforded by working with this extraordinary woman. From her, I learned two important lessons. First, it is only when we are comfortable with ourselves — our gender, race, position and so on — that we can be comfortable with those who are different from us. And second, for individuals to be successful, mutual respect for others must be the cornerstone of their operating philosophy.

These premises act like the two batteries necessary to turn on some flashlights. Once we create an awareness that this point of light begins within ourselves, we can begin to see our way to effectively manage diversity in other areas. Managing diversity means creating an atmosphere that internally and externally highlights the value of this asset.

To do this within an organization means striving to create an organization that:

1. Accepts individual and group differences and works to value all differences.

2. Utilizes these differences to achieve goals, and keeps everyone focused on those goals.

3. Encourages communication.

4. Pulls everyone together, integrating each individual into the organization as a whole. Individual teams, groups, or departments should not be allowed to break away and isolate themselves from others.

5. Is characterized by mutual respect.

6. Allows each individual to speak for herself or himself.

MOVING TOWARD DIVERSIFIED WHOLENESS

Whether approached from the direction of socio-political correctness, performance issue, ethical imperative, or business strategy, the sought-for destination is a sense of wholeness.

This wholeness is the understanding that is created when individuals and organizations experience a sense of oneness about who they are, what they are doing, how they are doing it, and where they are headed in the future. Differences can create a special kind of completeness, allowing all concerned to better understand who they are as individuals and as part of the organization.

Earlier in this chapter I told about my experiences as a young basketball player and the importance of using the diverse skills of everyone on the team to "go for the rim." In a broad sense, the importance of diversity is similar in the workplace as we daily try to get the job done. And just as the young men on that basketball team felt a real sense of oneness as they huddled together, sweated together, went through wins and losses together, creating this sense of oneness in the workplace promotes the same sense of trust, dependence and effectiveness. Positions shift from defensive to offensive as each of us brings our differences onto a common court, so that we can become better at understanding. While diversity may react out of demographic and social projections and is influenced by competitive pressures, it is ultimately the affirmation of the different talents and gifts we all bring to that larger game of life.

WORDS FROM WYNCOM

"One thing I've had to adjust to is the 'family' that works together. I've learned to be more tolerant." — *Terri Cecil*

"Working with people whose backgrounds and life experiences are significantly different from mine continually challenges me to learn to see the world from their perspective and find the aspects of their culture which will help make me a better person and employee." — *Maureen Baxter*

"Differences have enhanced my life through offering alternatives to consider. Every person has something to positively (and negatively) offer. I try to focus on the positive offering of the diversity of life. Diversity affects my work with other people in that diversity allows me the opportunity to practice 'acceptance' in my life. I work hard to accept others' beliefs as their own without allowing my own beliefs to be dampened. . . . I listen to input when it is offered." — *Carolyn Coffey*

"I've never met a person who wasn't significantly different from me. I think these differences make work more interesting. Not always easy, but never boring. As long as people respect my age, background and experiences, we can work together." — *Gretchen Witham*

"WYNCOM is a 'melting pot,' and it has been nothing less than fantastic working with all the age, background, ethnic and other differences. I love them all — what a family!" — *Doug Richard*

"I have met some great people, and I have met some people that I generally would not be close, personal friends with, as well. I have grown as a person because I have had to go up and beyond the normal call of duty to be personal and close with these individuals. I realize that if I do not sacrifice myself and my own selfish desires that it not only hurts me, but it hurts the other individuals and the company as a whole." — *Scott Via*

"We have a very diverse management team at WYNCOM, with very different styles. My style is very different from Larry's. Larry is not a detail person, but much more of a global idea person. He surrounds himself with people who effectively bring the details to order and get them executed efficiently. I think Larry is a forward thinker, looking out several steps beyond today. I'm more of a detail person, though not quite at the level of Rose Cord, the Chief Operating Officer and Chief Financial Officer. My style is more accepting of a lot of inputs. I have good skills at negotiation and presentation that maybe some don't. I think we all have strengths, and we all have weaknesses, but overall, that creates a complementary set of skills."
— *Jerry Miller*

95 ways to create and benefit from diversity

1. Actively encourage diversity in your company. People from different backgrounds and with different perspectives will invigorate your company.

2. Bring more women into management. Women often have a different take on things, a new perspective that can benefit the company.

3. Learn to be a good listener. By listening carefully to diverse opinions, you can learn to appreciate the value of diversity.

4. Promote diversity as a means of promoting understanding among employees.

5. Create procedures in your company that encourage all employees to offer ideas and solutions to problems.

6. Share more of who you are and your perspective with your co-workers. Be more than your job description or title.

7. When organizing teams, committees or work groups, include different perspectives. Make sure groups are balanced with representatives from several (if not all) functional areas of the organization. Also include people of different ages and backgrounds.

8. Develop a mindset that recognizes diversity as profitable. The more different people who are involved in the company, the broader the perspective — and the greater the potential.

9. Maintain a healthy cynicism toward your own knowledge. As Socrates said, "I know nothing except the fact of my ignorance." *Everyone* has something to teach you — from the CEO to the line worker to the custodian. Talk to people, whoever they are.

10. Put your commitment to diversity in writing. If your company has a mission or belief statement, make sure that it supports diversity.

11. Volunteer. Participating in community service helps you see new possibilities. Skills learned in volunteer positions can often carry over into your profession.

12. Expand your circle of friends and associates. Get to know individuals who are different — perhaps very different — from you.

13. Read contemporary literature from different cultures. Pick up a book by a living Russian, Japanese or African author.

14. Seek out the advice of older persons. Listen to the stories of their experiences.

15. Learn to see an issue from the perspective of others. Henry Ford said: "If there is any one secret of success it lies in the ability to get the other person's point of view and see things from his angle as well as from your own."

16. Encouraging diversity can enhance and develop creativity. Allow yourself to look at the world in a way that is open to all possibilities.

17. Develop and enhance your interpersonal skills. As the world grows smaller in the decades to come, your ability to get along with and understand others will become vital to your success.

18. Learn to consider alternatives in every situation. Think in terms of "relative" rather than "absolute" facts.

19. Encourage free discussion of ideas. Successful organizations are those where workers are not afraid to express their opinions. Remember: Today's off-the-wall idea may be next month's best-selling product.

20. Develop programs in the workplace in such areas as communication, negotiation, problem solving and conflict resolution.

21. Help team members learn and understand the skills and responsibilities of their co-workers. This helps create empathy as well as flexibility. It increases everyone's sense of self-worth, belonging and making a positive contribution.

22. Learn a foreign language. Denis Waitley in *Empires of the Mind* recounts a standard joke from Japan: What do you call someone who speaks three languages? Answer: Tri-lingual. Two languages? Bi-lingual. One language? American! Become the exception.

23. Attend cultural events or classes to learn more about different countries. In today's rapidly changing world, you never know where your market may be tomorrow.

24. Keep your ego in check by weighing the advice of diverse viewpoints.

25. Investigate the practices of top foreign business leaders. Read about the management styles of such leaders as Jacques Calvet of Peugeot (France), Hans Albers of BASF (Germany), and Shiro Egawa of Nippon Credit Bank (Japan).

26. Frequently have lunch or dinner in an ethnic restaurant. Sample authentic foods from other cultures — such as Indian, Vietnamese and Lebanese — that are new to you.

27. Introduce yourself to music from other cultures. You might begin by browsing in the "world beat" section of a large record shop.

28. Read *National Geographic* and watch public television for programs that offer insight into other countries and cultures.

29. Keep in mind that equal opportunity employment is the law. More important, it's good public relations. Even more important, it's the right thing to do. Most important, it's good for your company in more ways than you can possibly imagine.

30. Visit a church, temple or synagogue of a faith that's different from your own. Instead of focusing on the differences, look for the similarities.

31. Offer in-house culture and gender awareness classes to your employees so they can become better equipped to communicate effectively with people from diverse backgrounds.

32. Conduct an extensive survey of your customer base. Pay special attention to the diverse attributes of the people who patronize your business. What are their differences? What are their commonalities? Look for new and exciting ways to market your company to this diverse group.

33. Learn to stop identifying people by their gender, skin color or ethnic origin.

34. Develop a "mentoring" program that pairs younger employees with older ones. While the veterans share their knowledge, experience and wisdom, they can also benefit from the curiosity and enthusiasm of youth.

35. Hire people with special needs to do odd jobs for the organization. They are likely to attack their assignments with enthusiasm and will quickly gain confidence and competence. Everyone benefits. Local community-service organizations may be able to put you in touch with appropriate job candidates.

36. Encourage employees to contribute a percentage of their work week to volunteer causes. In addition to having a positive effect on the community, this work will broaden the volunteers' perspective (and help build goodwill for your organization in the community).

37. Consider Stephen Covey's interpretation of the Golden Rule, as explained in *The Seven Habits of Highly Effective People*: "The Golden Rule says to 'Do unto others as you would have others do unto you.' While on the surface that could mean to do for them what you would like to have done for you, I think the more essential meaning is to understand them deeply as individuals, the way you would want to be understood, and then to treat them in terms of that understanding. As one successful parent said about raising children, 'Treat them all the same by treating them differently.'"

38. Offer incentives for employees to enroll in sociology classes and other courses that promote understanding and tolerance for other cultures and lifestyles. Any continuing education course, in fact, is likely to help employees develop their personal knowledge bases.

39. Talk to current employees about any concerns they might have regarding organizational diversity initiatives. If they feel resentful or threatened, encourage them to voice their opinions so you can discuss them openly.

40. Give employees the opportunity to grow professionally and advance within the company, adding to the diversity of their skills.

41. Hold an annual talent show that allows employees to share diverse talents — such as singing, dancing, juggling, poetry or magic — that might not be apparent on the job.

42. Read differing accounts of historical events, especially those written from the perspective of the oppressed.

43. Develop a "stereotype sensor" that allows you to detect — and move beyond — prejudices and preconceptions.

44. Work at realizing the value of the *second* impression. Give someone another chance.

45. It's amazing how much you can accomplish if you don't care who gets the credit. Try letting go of an idea, allowing other people to play with it for a while and put their own unique stamp on it. There's a very good chance that the idea which returns to you will be stronger than the one you originally conceived.

46. Take a trip to another country. Instead of gravitating toward those places where English is spoken, go where the locals congregate. Get a feel for what it's like to be a "foreigner."

47. Participate in community groups that are actively seeking solutions to racial conflict and other problems that result from a lack of understanding.

48. Make sure that project teams contain both "big picture" thinkers and detail-oriented people.

49. If possible, participate in an employee exchange program with an overseas company in your field.

50. Build a company library with a diversity of business and management literature, as well as stimulating fiction from a variety of cultures.

51. Provide cross-training opportunities so employees can fill in for one another during vacations, emergencies and other unexpected situations. Cross-training also helps employees understand the interdependence of each role, and how each contributes to the overall operation.

52. When filling part-time positions, consider the fact that many retirees are looking for something to do and are eager to make a contribution. Their accumulated wisdom, as well as their enthusiasm about re-entering the workforce, can yield great benefits.

53. Develop a deeper understanding of the uniqueness of cultures that many people tend to "lump together." For example, there may be many similarities between various Latin American countries, but each has its own unique characteristics. The same holds true for Asian countries.

54. Make your workplace accessible to customers — and employees — with disabilities. Take steps to hire talented people who refuse to see their physical condition as limiting.

55. If your organization is unionized, build an atmosphere of trust between the union and management. Focus on common goals, not differences. Be sure to keep the union informed of diversity issues as they arise.

56. Appreciate the diversity of youth. Avoid catch-all phrases like "Generation X" that attempt to pigeonhole all people of a certain age into one homogeneous category.

57. Creating a diverse workplace doesn't mean simply bringing in people with diverse backgrounds and skill levels,

then leaving them on their own to sink or swim. Help them develop into productive employees who work well with others and want to grow with the organization. Diversity training can include multicultural integration workshops, cross-cultural communication skills and more. These training sessions should benefit not only the new hires but also others throughout the organization — in short, everyone who is affected.

58. In order to properly educate people about gender and racial issues, communication is needed. Create ample opportunities for employees to get together in groups and express their feelings to one another. Encourage them to forget about being "politically correct" and speak what's on their minds. Then it will be much easier not only to develop understanding but also to address problem areas.

59. *Celebrate* differences rather than denying them or trying to force everyone into a particular mold. Realize the uniqueness of each individual — and the potential for combining these unique attributes in powerful and exciting new ways.

60. Know yourself. Analyze your own background and upbringing. Did you grow up with biases toward certain groups of people, whether based on gender, skin color, religion or something else? If so, consider how you were shaped by this upbringing and how you can overcome these prejudices. The key to overcoming prejudice is first being aware of it.

61. Keep your eyes and ears open for generalizations — the source of stereotypes. Realize that, even within a certain category, the members are themselves unique. Avoid blanket statements which imply that everyone within a group behaves the same way.

62. Look for talent in non-traditional and unorthodox places. Instead of automatically looking for someone with a business-school degree, consider hiring someone who hasn't graduated from college but who is talented, aggressive and full of exciting new ideas.

63. Visit minority colleges and job fairs in search of potential job candidates.

64. Talk to people from other organizations that have been successful in creating diverse workforces. Find out their "secrets," which they will probably be happy to share.

65. Become more aware of gender-based communication styles. By doing so, you can make allowances rather than take the disparities personally. The better we understand differences, the better our chances of bridging communication gaps.

66. Learn sign language. Use it whenever you get an opportunity. In addition to giving you the ability to communicate with hearing-impaired people, this new skill will help you communicate more effectively with body language.

67. Select a diverse group of role models for personal and organizational motivation. Encourage employees to contribute their lists of biggest influences for publication in the company newsletter or posting on the bulletin board.

68. Teach someone to speak English.

69. Do your part to create an organizational culture that welcomes change and is not afraid of the unknown.

70. Create a scholarship or internship program for high school or college students from disadvantaged backgrounds who are interested in your profession. Form a mentoring program with employees from your company to work with disadvantaged high school students.

71. Consult women, blacks and members of other minority groups to find ways to make your products and services more appealing to members of those groups.

72. Hold occasional social events, away from the workplace, where employees and their families can get together and *really* get to know one another.

73. Help your organization develop relationships with diverse *outside* groups. Consider forming partnerships (formal or

informal) with individuals and organizations that can lend a new perspective to your vision.

74. Recognize the diversity of today's lifestyles by providing opportunities for flexible work situations such as "flex-time" or working from home. Many talented and creative people are looking for jobs that offer an alternative to the traditional 9-to-5, at-the-office routine.

75. Welcome alternative solutions. Employing a diversity of thinking styles requires that you be open to the fact that there's generally more than one way to do a job or solve a problem. Welcome new solutions that may be better than the old ones. Keep in mind the words of Teddy Roosevelt: "The best executives are the ones who have sense enough to pick good men to do what they want done, and self-restraint enough to keep from meddling with them while they do it." (Of course, let's change "good men" to "good people.")

76. Conduct a diversity audit of your organization. In what areas are you succeeding? In what areas do you need to improve? Identify problems, shortcomings, barriers and misunderstandings, and then take the necessary steps to correct them.

77. Use the company newsletter or other medium to regularly communicate information about diversity to employees. Make sure everyone realizes the importance of a diverse workforce.

78. Make it clear to all employees that harassment, hostility or other intolerant behavior has no place in the workplace. Discipline those who do not cooperate. Terminate those who consistently refuse to cooperate.

79. Eat lunch with someone you ordinarily don't eat lunch with. This person could be someone from a different department, someone of the opposite sex, someone of a different race, or someone whose way of thinking differs from you. Listen to what this person has to say about work and life.

80. If you unintentionally offend a co-worker with something you do or say, find out *why* this person was offended and how you can prevent similar occurrences in the future.

81. Compile a resource library of newspaper and magazine articles, books and videotapes on diversity and related issues. Encourage employees to use these resources to become more educated about diversity.

82. Form a diversity committee that will meet regularly to discuss the organization's progress toward diversity goals and ways to keep everyone informed. The committee — which should comprise a representative sample of employees — could also play a key role in helping resolve any disputes or problems that might arise.

83. Do a regular analysis of turnover rates in your organization. Are there any groups where the rate is disproportionately high? If so, this may be a sign that the organization needs to study how people from these groups are treated on the job.

84. Recognize that diversity comes in many forms. Some are cultural, while others are cognitive, or related to the way people process information. People differ from one another in many ways, including age, gender, race, ethnic origin, language, religion, educational background, sexual orientation, lifestyle, status as a military veteran, physical ability, mental ability, political outlook and thinking style.

85. Periodically ask employees about their perceptions of the organization. How comfortable are they with their co-workers? Do they feel accepted for themselves, especially if they are "different" or "unconventional"? Do you feel encouraged to grow and strive to reach their full potential? Do they feel involved and a part of things, including decision making? Are they rewarded for their achievements?

86. Look at the diversity of your products and services. Could your organization benefit by expanding into new markets or customizing existing products and services to a particular

group? "Older" Americans, for example, represent one of the most powerful purchasing groups — a fact that is often overlooked in the youth marketing frenzy.

87. Be sure that senior management supports the organization's diversity initiatives, in action, not just in theory. Without real support from the top, any efforts will probably stall.

88. Realize that creating, educating and maintaining a diverse workforce will cost money. Specifically budget for these initiatives, which if properly executed will bring an excellent return on investment.

89. When hiring people to work for you, refrain from hiring "yes" men and women. Instead, look for people who aren't afraid to disagree with you and suggest alternatives to your ideas. As the journalist Walter Lippman said, "Where all think alike, no one thinks very much."

90. Be realistic in your planning. A diverse workforce cannot be created overnight. Establish short- and long-term goals, then constantly measure your progress toward those goals.

91. Take an active role in the education of the young. Many school systems have developed programs in which businesses partner with individual schools to provide equipment, knowledge and other resources. Remember: Today's children are tomorrow's leaders.

92. Make sure that "more women and minorities in upper management" is one of your goals. *Every* level of the organization should have the opportunity to benefit from diversity.

93. Go where the action is. Visit Pacific Rim countries and other areas where new standards are being set in productivity and innovation. Be open-minded and willing to learn from overseas success stories.

94. Get out of your ivory tower and into the "real world" on a regular basis. It's easy to become insulated and lose touch with what's happening at the grassroots level. Travel frequently, domestically and abroad, and talk to the people who are

on the front lines, making things happen. What they have to say might surprise you.

95. Look for a mosaic, not a melting pot. Consider the editorial from an Alabama Baptist newsletter: "A mosaic is a design of some kind formed by every minute piece of glass, stone or something else which is inlaid in a ground of stucco or metal, all of which are different, yet they blend into a complete whole. Thus the symbol of our nation is rather that of a mosaic than a melting pot. A melting pot enforces conformity, and our rule as a nation should be and is to make use of differences to create a worthy whole."

For further reading . . .

Carr, Clay. *The Competitive Power of Constant Creativity* (Amacom). Chapter 4, "How to Use Diversity and Conflict Creatively," provides a helpful definition of diversity, argues for the benefits of diversity in organizations, and suggests ways to deal constructively with the conflicts that sometimes result from diversity.

Chappell, Tom. *The Soul of a Business* (Bantam). Chapter 7, "Intentional Diversity: Creating Complex Beauty," is an especially thoughtful discussion of the importance of diversity at Tom's of Maine. Drawing heavily on analogies from psychology and biology, the chapter ends with Chappell's vision of "the company as a diverse ecosystem."

Gentile, Mary C., ed. *Differences that Work: Organizational Excellence through Diversity* (Harvard Business Review). This collection of *HBR* articles on diversity in the workplace pays special attention to racial diversity, gender differences and AIDS issues.

Gray, John. *Men Are from Mars, Women Are from Venus* (Harper Collins). This best-selling discussion of the differences between men and women in behavior, emotions and communication styles offers detailed suggestions for improving male-female relationships, in and out of the workplace. "Reality," includes, on page 108, good suggestions for incorporating diverse, even dissenting, views into corporate visions.

Griggs, Lewis Brown, and Lente-Louise Louw. *Valuing Diversity: New Tools for a New Reality* (McGraw-Hill). Offering new perspectives from consultants and clients working with diversity, the Griggs-Louw approach emphasizes both personal transformation and systemic change as the basis for a strong diversity program. An acclaimed film/video training series of the same name has also been produced by the authors.

Harris, Herbert W. *Racial and Ethnic Identity: Psychological Development and Creative Expression* (Routledge). This collection of essays, developed from a conference held at Yale University on the subject of racial and ethnic identity, focuses on the idea that race and ethnicity comprise only a single aspect of the identity of the individual.

Kouzes, James M., and Barry Z. Posner. *Credibility: How Leaders Gain and Lose it, Why People Demand it.* (Jossey-Bass). Chapter 4, "Appreciating Constituents and Their Diversity," offers excellent insights into the value of diversity for effective leadership and for enriching performance through diversity.

Peters, Tom. *The Pursuit of WOW! Every Person's Guide to Topsy-Turvy Times* (Vintage). "The Diversity Advantage," beginning on page 219, is a dialogue with associates from Federal Express in Memphis that highlights the author's belief that diversity is an awesome opportunity as opposed to a problem.

Pollar, Odette, and Rafael Gonzalez, *Dynamics of Diversity: Strategic Programs for Your Organization* (Crisp Publications). This book uses a variety of approaches to assist companies in addressing the issue of designing and implementing a successful, ongoing diversity program.

Schwarz, Benjamin. "The Diversity Myth: America's Leading Export." *Atlantic Monthly* (May 1995). This article refutes the idea that America has a history of ethnic tolerance and multicultural harmony. This article provides insight into understanding where we as individuals, as organizations and as a nation need to direct our efforts toward diversity.

Simons, George. *Working Together: How to Become More Effective in a Multicultural Workplace* (Crisp Publications). This book offers insights for leaders to build diversity awareness and skills.

Waitley, Denis. *Empires of the Mind: Lessons to Lead and Succeed in a Knowledge-Based World* (Morrow). Chapter 6, "Self-Leadership and Vision: Your Virtual Reality," emphasizes that the need for diversity begins with individual self-knowledge and leadership.

Walton, Sally. *Cultural Diversity in the Workplace* (Mirror Press). This book highlights the rapid changes that are taking place in the workforce and suggests how organizations need to take advantage of these changes.

GET
THINGS
DONE

CHAPTER

I don't have time."

"I'll get to it when this project is completed."

"I'll try."

"Who has time for that?"

No doubt you've heard all of these comments about time, and have probably uttered them yourself when the pressure was on. While we all experience the occasional "crush," many of our problems with time can be addressed by making a serious study of time management. In this chapter, you'll get a good start toward being more productive, taking control of your day — and taking control of your life. We'll also take a look at the problem-solving process as it relates to innovation.

In *The Seven Habits of Highly Effective People*, Stephen Covey advises to "Begin with the End in Mind." He's referring to proper planning and a clear idea of completed work. It's an excellent way to go about accomplishing a goal or completing a task. In the years just after I started my own business, I drove thousands of miles to meet potential customers. When I got in my car in Lexington, Kentucky, I certainly couldn't look down the block and see an office building in Chicago. But if I headed in the right direction, made the necessary course corrections and just kept going, I knew I would get there. The principle works, whether you're driving the family car on a vacation or tackling a big project at work.

Unfortunately, some people are so frightened or confused by big projects that they have trouble beginning at all. "It's too big a job. I'll never get it done on time," they say. Or even more often, they say, "I just don't know where to begin."

If you practice good, strong self-leadership, you'll recognize that the beginning of the project is wherever you say it is! Your first idea may not be a big part of the final product, but it is a start, and that's what you're searching for at a time when a big project looks so intimidating.

> "Time is totally irreplaceable. Within limits, we can substitute one resource for another, copper for aluminum, for instance. We can substitute capital for human labor. We can use more knowledge or more brawn. But there is no substitute for time."
> — Peter Drucker, *The Effective Executive*

In *Sales Secrets from Your Customers*, Barry J. Farber offers some good tips for getting started when you're "stalled."

"Try the 'do one more' principle," Farber writes. "Whenever things start getting tough or an obstacle appears, there is one thing you can do that doesn't take any kind of special talent, and that is work a little bit harder. Stay one extra hour. Make one more phone call. Write one more thank-you note. Do just one more activity than you think you can. Customers will sense that extra effort, and it will pay off in the end."

If you need another incentive, use what I call the 10-minute rule. Tell yourself that you will spend the next 10 minutes working on the project. If you can complete 10 minutes of work, your self-imposed rules will allow you to stop and move on to something else if you want. I still use the 10-minute rule on occasion, and I can tell you that I have never stopped working after only 10 minutes. The energy lift you will feel just by getting started at all is amazing. In almost every case, you will continue working productively on the troublesome project for a far longer period, feeling better and better about your work as you go.

Here are five steps that will help you get things done, and done well:

1. Think

2. Outline

3. Draft

4. Revise

5. Move ahead

Think.

The boss enters an office and finds an employee staring out the window.

"What are you doing?" the boss asks.

"Just thinking," the employee replies.

"Well, cut it out and get back to work," the boss roars. "We don't have time for that around here!"

It may be a high-tech world, and I'm all for making good use of modern technology, but don't discount the old-fashioned methods. In his classic personal development audio cassette series, *Lead the Field*, the late Earl Nightingale recommended taking one hour a day, five days a week, to exercise the mind.

"You don't even have to do it on weekends," Nightingale said. "Pick one hour a day that you can count on fairly regularly. The best time for me is an hour before the others are up in the morning. The mind is clear, the house is quiet, and, if you like, with a fresh cup of coffee, this is the time to start the mind going."

A quiet house, a fresh cup of coffee — what a great setting to do some great thinking! I like to take an occasional long weekend at the beach in North Carolina. Add the sound of the ocean waves to the setting that Earl Nightingale described, and you have my prescription for productive thinking.

You certainly don't have to be at the beach to think, but you do need to find that time and place where your mind can go to work without interruption.

Break through the barrier that has caused thinking time to be labeled "idle" time. It's just the opposite! Find the time to think, and record your ideas. You may discover that over the long term, you'll be more productive during that period than at any time during the day.

Merrill E. Douglass and Donna N. Douglass, authors of *Manage your Time, Your Work, Yourself,* remind us that much can be accomplished in short increments.

"Do not be overly concerned if you do not have much time each day to devote to your goals. Even fifteen minutes a day can make a tremendous difference in your life. In fifteen minutes a day, you can learn a foreign language, trace your family history, learn to play a musical instrument, or read a good book. Fifteen minutes a day add up to over ninety hours each year. That's the equivalent of two full work weeks. Minutes do count. If you use them wisely, they can make a big difference in the quality of your life."

> "Dost thou love life? Then do not squander time; for that's the stuff life is made of."
> — Benjamin Franklin

That's especially true if you're using those minutes do some high-quality thinking. More from Earl Nightingale:

"During this hour every day, take a completely blank sheet of paper. At the top of the page, write your present primary goal – clearly, simply. Then, since our future depends upon the way in which we handle our work, write down as many ideas as you can for improving that which you do now. Try to think of 20 possible ways in which the activity that fills your day can be improved. You won't always get 20, but even one idea is good."

You're probably facing a situation right now — a project at work, a job search, a personal problem — in which you could use one good idea. Do you really think you'll come up completely empty if you set aside that regular time to think hard about the problem?

Outline.

Once the ideas begin to come, you'll need to organize them. The principle of breaking a big job down into several smaller ones has long been effective in fighting procrastination and a lack of productivity. Again, you don't need to have the final destination in sight. You just need to know you're moving in the right direction. Many people report feeling real physical relief after they've organized a project into smaller segments.

Make an outline, just as you did in grade school, with major topics I, II and III and subtopics A, B, C and so on. With each division of tasks, the entire job will seem less intimidating. Set deadlines for completing each segment of the job.

Draft.

Get ideas down on paper, or into a computer. You'll be more organized, and you'll feel much better about the entire project because your notes will be a tangible "product" of your work.

Perfectionism often appears at some point in this process. How long will it take you to be perfect? How much time will you consume by trying to do perfect work? Do you think perfection is a realistic goal? Of course it isn't!

Concentrate on doing your best work, not perfect work. If you've found time to think, you will arrive at your best work much quicker than if you agonize over work that is less than perfect.

> "Effective executives, in my observation, do not start with their tasks. They start with their time. And they do not start out with planning. They start by finding out where their time actually goes. Then they attempt to manage their time and to cut back unproductive demands on their time. Finally they consolidate their 'discretionary' time into the largest possible continuing units. This three-step process: recording time; managing time; and consolidating time is the foundation of executive effectiveness."
>
> — Peter Drucker, *The Effective Executive*

What if you're just not in the right frame of mind? Merrill and Donna Douglass have some excellent advice for beating a bad mood.

"There is usually some aspect of the task that will fit your current mood. You may not feel like papering the kitchen today, but you might at least be willing to select the wallpaper. . . . Ask yourself, 'Is there anything, no matter how small, that I am willing to do?' Once you find something you're willing to do — and do it — you're on the way to making your moods work for instead of against you."

Keep a notepad or a recorder with you so that good ideas won't be lost. You can organize them at a later time, but the simple act of writing or recording them will let you know you are indeed at work, and as long as you are coming up with good ideas, you are in fact making good progress toward completion of the work, just as I was making good progress on my cross-country drives.

Revise.

Now you're ready for some fine tuning. You've already divided the entire project into smaller segments — now just divide the segments. You'll find that many of the solutions have already occurred to you (because you've been thinking). By this stage, you'll be looking at the details that will complete the job. This is also a good time to make sure that anyone else who has to be involved is up to date. If WYNCOM uses an outside company to print a publication, for example, all our efforts toward completing the copy won't do us much good if we're not on the printer's calendar in time to meet our deadline.

Move ahead.

Break through your comfort zone, and cut down cycle times. I enjoy watching the reactions of WYNCOM employees when they view a video produced by the San Diego Homebuilders Association in which a house is constructed from start to finish in less than three hours!

Yes, it is possible! It wouldn't be practical to build every house in three hours, but if it is possible under the right circumstances, do you think a "three-month" project could be done in two months? Wouldn't an extra *month* be valuable to you and your company?

WYNCOM headquarters is located in a historic building near downtown Lexington, Kentucky. In early 1994, we occupied only part of the second floor of the building. As the company grew rapidly, we began to look elsewhere for additional office space. One day, several employees decided to tour the third floor of the building, which at that time was an unused attic. (Unused by humans, that is. Pigeons had been making use of it for some time, and their "productivity" didn't exactly leave a great working environment.)

At the same time our employees were making their tour, the building owners appeared, and they also wanted to take a look at that third floor. Since few of our employees had ever even seen the owners in the building, we took advantage of the moment and began discussions on the spot about renovating the third floor.

In February 1994, the project was launched. Our goal was to have the work completely done by April 20, at which time Stephen Covey was scheduled to appear in Lexington at a WYNCOM-sponsored program. We wanted Dr. Covey to tour our facilities, and we wanted him to see a completed project – comfortable, well-equipped offices open for business.

We had two and a half months to go from pigeon roost to business environment. Extraordinary teamwork was required of the landlord, architects, building manager, construction manager, interior designer, cabinet makers and audiovisual experts. It was close, but we made it! Dr. Covey made his visit, and the feeling of teamwork and accomplishment among our employees was evident as he toured the building. For many WYNCOM employees, the comfort zone had been greatly expanded. What at first seemed impossible had become reality.

INNOVATION AND PROBLEM SOLVING

Innovation is a continuous process — not a "been there, done that" event. Today's most innovative companies must continue their creative thinking, or they will be tomorrow's dinosaurs. Resting on today's successes is not an option.

Consider these examples of limited thinking that led to obsolescence, and of companies that succeeded because they were able to think creatively in new areas:

- No stagecoach company ever became a major railroad, no buggy producer a major automaker, no railroad a major bus company, and no railroad or bus company a major aircraft company. Yet if these companies had seen themselves as being in the *transportation* business rather than taking a more limited view, they would have been innovators.

- The most successful innkeeper in the world, Holiday Inn, was not started by experienced hotel people.

- Underwood didn't see IBM's electric typewriter as a serious competitive threat.

- Chrysler didn't react fast enough to the decline of the "gas guzzler," and, until recently, many other U.S. automakers suffered from the same problem.

We can look at innovation as problem solving. Often, innovative individuals and organizations solve "problems" before the rest of the world even realizes such problems exist.

While the problems, or challenges, that we face are becoming increasingly more sophisticated, the basic problem-solving process hasn't changed. The following step-by-step process is widely accepted in a variety of disciplines:

1. **Problem sensing (or problem awareness).** We need to sharpen our abilities to sense problems as they begin to appear. Being sensitive to changing conditions can result in the detection of a problem before it gets out of hand.

2. **Gathering the relevant data.** Once a problem is sensed, take time to gather any data about the problem.

3. **Defining the problem.** All too often, we tend to focus on the symptoms instead of the problem, simply

because we don't take enough time to think about the ultimate cause. A good technique for arriving at the root problem is to define it initially and then ask, "Is this the real problem, or is there a deeper problem at work?" When no deeper problem can be identified, then perhaps the main problem has been defined.

4. **Listing alternative solutions.** List as many possible solutions as we can. At this point, don't throw out the "silly" solutions, because they can often lead to better ones. This step and the previous one call for creative thinking, but unfortunately one or both steps are often skipped.

5. **Selecting the best solution.** The chances of finding a good solution to a problem are much better when adequate time has been spent on the first four steps. Overlooking or underestimating important steps often leads to the same old solutions, which never seem to work quite well enough.

6. **Taking action.** No matter how impressive the groundwork is, there is no benefit if no action is taken (unless it's one of those cases in which no action is actually the best solution). Once you've found the solution, employ it!

Problems are the lifeblood of innovation. Find a problem, figure out how to solve it, and you are being innovative! Talk about getting things done!

WORDS FROM WYNCOM

"Deadlines are overrated. Stress, sleepless nights and worry come from not believing in your personnel and yourself. Meeting a deadline has nothing to do with stress and heartache, but rather, it has to do with dedication and commitment to themselves and a job well done."
— *Scott Via*

"I get things done by setting goals. I have two lists. Short term and long term. My long-term list consists of goals I hope to accomplish in one to six months. I try to accomplish short-term goals in a day or up to a week. I make lists of my goals, mark them on my calendar, make myself notes, anything to help me remember. Then I prioritize them — I put my most important goals at the top of the lists and work my way down." — *Melissa Fightmaster*

"Time management is the key. I believe that first we need to access our goals. After we know what our goal is, we need to find the most profitable route to go to achieve that goal." — *Kyle Bixler*

"Prioritize! Usually by the day, sometimes by the hour and on occasion by the minute!" — *Marty Adcock*

"Which alligator has the most teeth? What is the priority?" — *Tyra Swilo*

"I try to set my own personal deadlines to be a week ahead of the real deadline. This allows for any last-minute, time-consuming problems that might come up."
— *Doug Richard*

"Teamwork, teamwork, teamwork. Database Administration has a superb group of team players whose goal is to produce quality work in an amiable, proficient and timely fashion. We all depend entirely on each other when we know the game plan. Then we begin to hammer away at our little piece of the project. Result = Deadlines met."
— *Anna Lee Ginter*

"I get things done by knowing exactly what my needs are. I then set goals, make lists, update and, finally, celebrate when my goals are reached." — *Pat Sebastian*

How to change people's minds

by Kenneth W. Davis

When I asked more than 100 business leaders, "What are your three biggest communication problems?" their number-two answer (after "speaking to a group") was "being persuasive in my speaking and writing." These leaders recognized that leadership means having a vision, communicating it to others, and influencing them to follow. Effective leaders need to know how to change minds.

To change minds, we can use either of two strategies: direct and indirect. Direct persuasion, dating from ancient Greece, is based on the assumption that our reader or listener is a reasonable person who will be persuaded by good reasons. To use direct persuasion, we simply state our position and list the reasons for it.

In school, when we learned to write papers based on thesis statements, we were using direct persuasion. A thesis statement is simply a statement of a position, to be supported by the rest of the paper. The following first paragraph of a letter to a U.S. senator ends with a thesis statement, which the rest of the letter (not printed here) goes on to support:

> As you know, the U.S. government has been purchasing dairy cattle from farmers since the middle of 1986. In my opinion, the whole-herd dairy buyout program, as it is called, is a mistake.

The other strategy, indirect persuasion, is also ancient in its use, but it has not often been formally taught. It is based on the assumption that our reader or listener has an opposing position that he or she may not easily give up. Confronting such a person may lead not to a changed mind but to a hardening of the original position. Indirect persuasion attempts to avoid this problem by creating an atmosphere of cooperation and mutual understanding.

To persuade indirectly, begin by stating the problem objectively and, especially, by stating the *opposing* position accurately. By doing so, you demonstrate that you are a fair person who can see things through your opponent's eyes.

Then go a step further: Acknowledge the circumstances in which your opponent's position is, in fact, the right one.

At this point, your relationship with your reader or listener should be firmly established, so you can safely proceed to state *your* position and the circumstances in which *it* is the correct one. Notice that you have not threatened or alienated your reader or listener by opposing his or her position; instead you have agreed with it — at least in certain circumstances. All you have done is shown that circumstances also exist in which *your* position is right.

With this balance established between the two positions, you can go ahead and tip things your way, by showing that the circumstances in which your position is the right one are the circumstances that exist now. Better still, you may be able to present your position as simply a modification of the opposing one, or suggest a combination of both positions.

The following memo, written several years ago, is a good example of indirect persuasion:

> Thank you for asking me to comment on Dwight's proposal that Casey and Evans begin direct mail-order sales of our product line.
>
> The proposal has obviously been carefully thought out; it includes impressive statistics on the profit potential of mail order sales and a detailed plan for building a mailing list and handling the shipment of orders.
>
> The proposal is a sound one. In these days of two-income families and busy schedules, consumers are finding it increasingly convenient to shop by mail. Moreover, those mail-order companies that have earned high brand-name recognition are enjoying the benefits of direct marketing.
>
> However, new companies just entering the mail-order industry — companies without existing recognition and reputation — are not doing well. Given the state of the economy and the high costs of printing and postage, this is not a good time for such companies to begin mail-order sales.
>
> Unfortunately, Casey and Evans is such a company. While we have a reputation among retailers for quality novelty items, that recognition does not extend to the consumer. I suggest, therefore, that Dwight's excellent proposal be postponed until economic conditions improve. Meanwhile, Casey and Evans should

begin to give our brand name greater prominence on our products. I believe that in the future we might well want to move into mail-order sales.

Whichever strategy you adopt, keep in the mind the eight "principles of persuasion" listed in Gary Blake and Robert W. Bly's book *Elements of Business Writing:*

- Gain your reader's attention in an appropriate manner.

- Awaken a need for an idea before presenting the idea.

- Stress benefits, not features.

- Use facts, opinions, and statistics to prove your case.

- Don't get bogged down in unnecessary details or arguments.

- Tell the reader what to do next.

- Before making a request, give the reader a reason to respond.

- Do not assume the reader has been persuaded by your argument.

With these principles, and the right strategy, you can be a more persuasive communicator. You can change minds.

95 tips for effectively managing your time

1. Make a daily "to do" list. Set priorities and stick to them.

2. Zero in on opportunities, not problems.

3. Every few months take the time to chronicle how you spend your time for a two- or three-day period. Check what you've done, then replace unimportant activities with important ones.

4. Keep an index card that lists your top-priority personal and business goals. Refer to it often.

5. Focus on one thing at a time.

6. Set aside time to reflect on your most important goals. Pick out the activities that would help you achieve these goals, then schedule the more important ones into your daily routine.

7. Remember that being a workaholic rarely means better productivity.

8. Teach yourself the art of delegation. Then master it.

9. Carry blank index cards to capture creative thoughts.

10. Free yourself of negative thoughts based on fear of the future. Negative thoughts are time robbers. Be confident that you can handle any situation that may come your way. You can defeat most of your fears simply by being optimistic.

11. Set aside a specific time frame to complete certain activities. If you have consistently been sidestepping an important activity, reserve a window of time for it and nothing else.

12. Don't waste time trying to be perfect. Ninety-percent perfection is about all we can expect to achieve on most tasks..

13. Keep your work area organized.

14. On tasks such as mail, messages and reading materials, practice the principle of "single-handling." Deal with the task

immediately instead of setting it aside for later and letting it clutter your desk.

15. Allow yourself a few minutes of "think" time every day.

16. Stick to your important goals until they are completed to your satisfaction.

17. Fatigue makes cowards of us all, so it's important to remember that more often than not, it is mental rather than physical. Never give in to fatigue. Fight it like the enemy it is.

18. Begin challenging tasks while your confidence is "up" from a recent success.

19. If you get bogged down, get back on track by asking yourself the question that Alan Lakein posed in his classic 1973 book, *How to Get Control of Your Time and Your Life*: What is the most important use of my time RIGHT NOW?

20. Clarify the purpose of a meeting before calling it.

21. Distribute a meeting agenda with time limits placed on each topic. Stick to the time limits — except in those instances where a topic needs more time than planned.

22. Start meetings at the scheduled time. Stragglers will quickly get the message.

23. Position your desk so that potential "drop-ins" are not encouraged by eye contact.

24. Stand to greet "interrupters" and remain standing until you are finished talking.

25. Encourage a policy in your work area that allows for 30 minutes each morning and 15 minutes near the end of the day to be off limits to interruptions — unless there is a true crisis.

26. Before you "interrupt" a fellow worker with a problem, write it down so it will be clear in your mind. Encourage your employees to use the same technique.

27. *Listen* when you have made yourself available as a listener.

28. Don't talk on the phone to family members during the day. By making efficient use of your time at work, you will get home to your family much earlier.

29. Avoid asking unimportant questions when you are short on time.

30. Concentrate!

31. Set your watch three minutes fast to ensure being on time for your appointments. Others will respect your time if you respect theirs.

32. Remember that all time is valuable. Have something to read or some index cards to jot down thoughts in case you get stuck waiting. Regard such times as opportunities to sit, relax and think.

33. Don't become obsessed with "time management." Develop a sense of humor to get you through trying times.

34. Time your errands efficiently.

35. Exercise regularly but sensibly. Time spent in moderate exercise can more than pay for itself in the resulting increase in our energy.

36. Don't overindulge in food or drink. This will avoid sluggishness and wasted time.

37. Get the proper amount of sleep. We are not saving time if we don't meet our body's sleep requirement.

38. Know what your "prime time" is each day, then use it for your most important and most creative work. Save your routine tasks for the times when you tend to be less alert.

39. Don't say yes when you really mean no.

40. Look at a crisis as an challenge. See it as an opportunity to come up with a new, possibly better way of doing something.

41. When the consequences of a poor decision on a certain matter aren't likely to be severe, make the decision immediately. This will save time for the well-thought-out planning required for critical decisions.

42. Don't check off a completed activity on your daily "to do" list until you have started the next one. This will help you maintain momentum.

43. Use the telephone when it will accomplish the same thing as walking to someone's office.

44. A strenuous change-of-pace activity often will refresh us more than physical relaxation.

45. Don't generate needless and excessive paper work.

46. Don't try to be a perfectionist on minor projects. Also, consider the price of perfectionism on some of your bigger, more-important projects.

47. When answering the telephone, always be friendly and courteous. However, through intonation and voice speed, convey the idea that you are busy. Do the same when calling "talkative" people for specific information.

48. Try stand-up meetings.

49. Always set aside a few minutes each day to completely relax your body and mind.

50. Do not attempt to get *all* the little things out of the way first. You may "unclutter" your mind, but you won't have time to complete the big things.

51. Discourage excessive chitchat or small talk when starting to write.

52. Choose only one or two good sources of written information for specific subjects, then read them and closely *review* the most-relevant ideas.

53. Develop checklists for all routine activities. Don't allow time to be lost because of oversights.

54. Keep stationery with you. This will enable you to keep up with personal correspondence when you are "stuck without anything to do."

55. Develop and *use* a tickler-file system that works for you — at home and at work.

56. Don't leave your work area until you have planned and organized the next day's schedule. Know exactly what you are going to start on the next day. This will do wonders for relaxing your mind while away from the job.

57. Set aside a certain time each day when you don't take phone calls.

58. Save only one period during the day to handle your mail. If it's so urgent that it has to be handled as soon as it arrives, you've probably already heard about it.

59. Make yourself "unavailable" for unimportant meetings.

60. Don't procrastinate by dreaming up trivial chores that don't need immediate attention.

61. Remember that execution is better than planning. But execution without planning will lead to failure.

62. Make haste slowly when working on important tasks.

63. Use a calendar when making important plans.

64. If you're not enjoying it, ask, "Why am I doing it?"

65. Make an appointment before you leave to see someone.

66. Establish set times for important daily routines.

67. If a particular task requires a block of time for uninterrupted concentration, *create* that block of time.

68. Don't waste time fretting when someone or something interrupts your concentration. Forget it, and go *immediately* back to the interrupted task.

69. Underline pertinent ideas in an important book, then review them periodically.

70. Question any guilt feelings you have after saying "no."

71. Sleep late on a weekend only if your body needs it. Too much sleep is as bad as too little sleep.

72. Use alarms to remind yourself of those little but necessary tasks at the exact minute they're due.

73. Learn to use dictating equipment.

74. Smile! It takes no extra time and much less physical energy than a frown. Smiling can also do wonders for your productivity and the productivity of those around you.

75. Have certain times each day when you close your office door. Idle "chitchatters" will get the message.

76. Develop and maintain beneficial recreational interests, and schedule them at regular time intervals. It's amazing how productive we can be when we have something definite to look forward to.

77. Write out instructions that are intended for more than one person. If the instructions are technical, write them down even if they are for just one person.

78. Never fill a job with an unsuitable employee just to relieve immediate pressure. There are definite limits to the motivation of an employee in the wrong job.

79. Don't just have "good questions" planned when interviewing job candidates. Also know what answers you're looking for.

80. Be gracious with people while being stingy with time.

81. Never hesitate to compliment work that is well done.

82. Spend adequate time answering "why" when giving instructions.

83. Limit the amount of television you watch.

84. Recognize and understand the difference between activity and accomplishment.

85. Enjoy what you do.

86. Never fear the quick passage of time. Remember, there is always enough time for the important things.

87. Be aware of ways you can capture worthwhile time-saving techniques.

88. Use reading (not TV news) to be informed of events that will be forgotten by tomorrow.

89. Closely and honestly examine your habits. Change them if necessary.

90. Schedule vacations well in advance.

91. Perform one small task that you have been putting off. Doing so will help you build momentum for other tasks.

92. Break overwhelming tasks into small pieces that can be sandwiched in at intervals.

93. Think on paper. Pencils are great inventions.

94. Take control of how you spend your time. Also, set your own deadlines. When you let others set your deadlines, your performance tends to be mediocre.

95. Don't embrace success. Keep pushing forward, even when you know you have a winner. Running that last lap often makes the difference.

For further reading . . .

Bliss, Edwin C. *Getting Things Done: The ABCs of Time Management* (Bantam). This classic time management guide is an alphabetically ordered list of brief tips, from "After-Action Reports" through "Files, Proliferation of" and "Paper Work, Cost of" to "Workaholic."

Burka, Jane B., and Lenora M. Yuen. *Procrastination: Why You Do It, What to Do About It* (Addison Wesley). Based on the clinical experience of two psychologists, this book offers advice on understanding and overcoming procrastination.

Covey, Stephen R., A. Roger Merrill and Rebecca R. Merrill. *First Things First: To Live, To Love, To Learn, To Leave a Legacy* (Simon & Schuster). This expansion of Habit 3 in *Seven Habits* explores the powerful concept of what Covey calls "Quadrant II Organizing," the process of focusing on important, but not urgent, activities.

Covey, Stephen R. *The Seven Habits of Highly Effective People* (Simon & Schuster). While Covey's entire book is about "getting things done," Habit 3, "Put First Things First: Principles of Personal Management," is particularly useful in its new approach to time management.

Deep, Sam, and Lyle Sussman. *Yes, You Can!* (Seminars by Sam Deep). Several lists in this book, including "Achieve Personal Goals" (page 43) and a number of time management lists beginning on page 203, include useful tips for getting things done.

Ellis, Albert, and William J. Knaus. *Overcoming Procrastination* (Signet). Based on Ellis' techniques of "rational-emotive therapy," this book provides a number of sound methods for overcoming procrastination that results from "self-downing," "low frustration tolerance" and "hostility."

Love, Sydney F. *Mastery and Management of Time* (Prentice Hall). Although this book was first published nearly 20 years ago, it remains useful, especially for its "instant locator" section, which indexes dozens of common time management problems.

Peters, Tom. *The Pursuit of WOW! Every Person's Guide to Topsy-Turvy Times* (Vintage). The chapter titled "Getting Things Done," beginning on page 27, is an iconoclastic discussion of the uses and misuses of power.

Reynolds, Helen, and Mary E. Tramel. *Executive Time Management: Getting 12 Hours' Work Out of an 8-Hour Day* (Spectrum). This book discusses the particular time-management needs of executives, with chapters focusing on finding time to plan, do paper work, decide, write, converse, confer, lead and take stock.

Scott, Dru. *How to Put More Time in Your Life* (New American Library). Scott's five-step time management program is helpful in its exploration of the "psychology of time," leading to discovery of your own "time management style."

Smith, Hyrum W. *The Ten Natural Laws of Successful Time and Life Management: Proven Strategies for Increased Productivity and Inner Peace* (Warner). This book, by the CEO of Franklin Quest Company, offers a time management approach based on such fundamental principles as "when your daily activities reflect your governing values, you experience inner peace," "to reach any significant goal, you must leave your comfort zone" and "give more and you'll have more."

Taylor, Harold L. *Making Time Work for You* (Dell). This time management book encourages readers to "develop a time management philosophy" and "develop a time policy."

Waitley, Denis. *Empires of the Mind: Lessons to Lead and Succeed in a Knowledge-Based World* (Morrow). Chapter 12, "Self-Leadership and Resilience: Misfortune's Master," takes a healthy, flexible approach to self-management skills. In this chapter, Waitley is particularly helpful in his approach to overcoming procrastination and maintaining a sense of humor as you do.

Waitley, Denis. *Timing Is Everything: Turning Your Seasons of Success into Maximum Opportunities* (Nelson). Chapter 7, "The Season for Making Plans," and Chapter 11, "The Season for Effort," include especially helpful advice.

IMPROVE PERFORMANCE THROUGH COOPERATION

CHAPTER

In the summer of 1995, a new movie, *Apollo 13*, commemorated the 25th anniversary of the famous space flight. Starring Tom Hanks, the movie captured the imagination of Americans as it played in sold-out theaters across the country. More than simply a retelling of history, the movie inspired viewers with its sense of exhilaration and pride that comes from working together toward a goal worth achieving.

The flight of Apollo 13 was beset by obstacles. An explosion on board forced a change of plans to land on the moon and shifted the mission into a frenzied endeavor to return the astronauts home safely. On the ground, mission control teams worked frantically to come up with alternatives that could replace damaged equipment. In the spacecraft, the three astronauts pooled talents, experience and energy to create a focused cohesive unit with one mission in mind. Only with the cooperation of everyone involved were the astronauts able to navigate their crippled capsule back to earth.

After seeing this movie, I couldn't help but make links between the personal performance and cooperation demonstrated in the movie and what we experience daily at WYNCOM. This seemed particularly fitting considering the scope and sheer number of projects that the company had determined to undertake for the year.

I got excited. I dubbed WYNCOM's endeavors "the miracle mission," and determined to encourage all associates to share and expand that vision.

I wanted to put the company on "miracle status." WYNCOM employees consistently have demonstrated extraordinary effort in all they do. Now I was eager to see if we could turn this up a notch, going beyond past accomplishments to realize even greater challenges. Research shows that the mind's resources are much more extensive than those we usually tap.

> "People are the principal asset of any company, whether it makes things to sell, sells things made by other people, or supplies intangible services."
> — J. C. Penney

If, for example, people use only 1 percent of their capabilities on a particular task, why not challenge them to go for 2 percent?

To do this, I involved a team pulled from every area of the company to come up with guidelines for such a goal. Sparked by the success of Apollo 13, we planned to inspire everyone to achieve his or her personal best while creating an unstoppable group energy that would take us forward.

WYNCOM's miracle mission was formulated around these points:

1. START WITH A MISSION PLAN. You need to know where you're going and how you're going to get there.

2. BE PREPARED TO JETTISON IT. When circumstances change, focus on moving in sync with that change.

3. ENGAGE THE IMAGINATION AND SPIRIT OF EVERYONE INVOLVED. Present a strong focus that creates the desire to be a part of a winning team. Encourage creativity and the opportunity to feel good about what you are doing. Get excited and have fun.

4. MAXIMIZE YOUR RESOURCES. Don't underestimate or overlook the material resources, as well as human resources, that are available. You may be surprised with what you can find.

5. ATTITUDE IS EVERYTHING. Focus on the positive — what you want to accomplish, not what you want to avoid. During the Apollo 13 crisis, one person at Mission Control said, "This could be the biggest disaster in NASA history," but another stated: "I choose to look at this as our finest hour."

6. PUT EGOS ASIDE AND DON'T FOCUS ON "SNAPSHOTS." You can do anything as long as you don't have to take the credit.

7. EVERYBODY HAS A ROLE TO PLAY. Only three men were in space, but countless others on the ground were doing their part to support the mission. There may only be one speaker at a presentation that WYNCOM produces, but it

may take as many as a hundred individuals to make that event possible.

8. FAILURE IS NOT AN OPTION. I touched on this idea in the preface. Commitment to the mission helps the team overcome obstacle after obstacle, especially when it's a life-or-death situation — and there are plenty of those in today's frantic business environment.

PERSON TO PERSON

Getting people behind goals like these creates a cooperative spirit that gets the job done in ways that could never be imagined by people working alone. The organization benefits on a number of levels: increased productivity, improved decision-making and problem-solving abilities, enhanced customer service, creative marketing, less need for rules and policies, more opportunity for feedback and conflict resolution.

As vital as cooperation is for the organization, even greater benefits can go to the individual. Perhaps most importantly, cooperation allows everyone to reap the rewards of improved personal performance by adding to each person's pride, confidence and self-esteem. These feelings allow people to know who they are and to acknowledge that what we do in our daily lives, particularly in the workplace, is important. Low self-esteem on the other hand, can stifle the creative process, inhibiting each person from speaking up. This can be extremely detrimental when a company is trying to be innovative and competitive.

Successful collaboration creates confident individuals who take pride in what they do. They feel comfortable in taking on tasks and are willing to do what is necessary to get the job completed. They are able to work with others in solving problems, secure that everyone's contributions will be respected.

Cooperation also creates a sense of commitment by getting everyone involved in the decision-making process. Working toward a common goal lets people get more done, brainstorm for better ideas in less time and have more fun doing it all.

Melissa Fightmaster, registration coordinator at WYNCOM, describes such benefits: "My personal performance has improved through cooperation with others, because I learned to be more patient, more open to others' ideas and more empathetic. At WYNCOM, it is obvious how much teamwork it takes to get the job done."

> "The man who lives for himself is a failure; the man who lives for others has achieved true success."
> — Norman Vincent Peale

Finally, cooperation gives the individual a sense of control over his or her life by fostering comparison rather than criticism from an autocratic superior. "When working with a team I consider how something can be done more quickly and effectively," says

WYNCOM employee Mary Kessler. "That is a much more positive teaching tool than being criticized by a supervisor or manager. It is much easier to recognize that someone else has better methods that can improve your own performance than it is to simply have to admit you are wrong."

Scott Via, database administration worker, puts it this way: "At one point of my life, I use to hang my head in disbelief when someone would criticize me. Since I've been at WYNCOM, I find it to be a way of improving myself for my own benefit and the benefit of the company. Now, I talk to the people who have been in my department the longest and ask them to be open and honest with me about my shortcomings. Their feedback has helped my performance improve day by day."

GOING WITH THE GEESE

Perhaps the best analogy I know that clarifies the importance of improving personal performance through cooperation has to do with the habits of geese. Yes, geese. After reading this comparison (from a speech given by Angeles Arrien at the 1991 Organizational Development Network, based on the work of Milton Olson), I knew that it needed to be reflected somewhere in this book. After you've read the following, look again at the cover of the book!

HABIT: With a flap of its wings each goose creates an "uplift" for the flock that follows. All the birds achieve 71 percent greater flying range by flying in a "V" formation than if each flew alone.

MORAL: Individuals who share a common direction and sense of community can reach their destination faster and easier by traveling on the thrust of one another.

HABIT: A goose that falls out of formation suddenly feels the drag and resistance of solo fight. It returns to formation as soon as possible to resume smooth flight by the lifting power of the bird immediately in front of it.

MORAL: If we are as sensible as geese we stay in formation with those headed where we want to go. We are willing accept their assistance and make our help available to others.

HABIT: As the lead goose becomes fatigued, it goes back into formation, allowing another goose to fly in the point position.

MORAL: It is to everyone's advantage to share leadership. People, like geese, depend on one another's abilities, energies and experiences.

HABIT: The geese following behind honk to encourage the leaders to keep up their speed.

MORAL: Honking must be encouraged. Production levels rise in groups where encouragement is given. Standing by one's values and supporting those of the group provide the type of honking we need.

HABIT: When a goose becomes ill or hurt, a pair of geese leave the formation and follow it to offer help and protection. They remain with it until the goose dies or recovers. Then they join another formation or catch up with the original flock.

MORAL: If we are as smart and sensitive as geese, we will stand by each other in good times and bad.

TOOLS FOR EMPATHY

The key to shared vision is incorporating each person's personal vision into the group vision. This process requires that channels be kept open for communication — upward, downward, and laterally.

To keep these channels open, everyone in the organization must practice empathy.

Building empathy involves three tools: **asking, listening** and **reinforcing.**

1. Ask.

In their book *Leaders: The Strategies for Taking Charge,* Warren Bennis and Burt Nanus write, "Successful leaders, we have found, are *great askers.*"

To be a "great asker," learn to ask "W and H" questions, not "yes-no" questions. That is, ask questions that begin with *Who, What, Where, When, Why* and *How.* Such questions require the other person to answer at greater length, and give you more information.

Make your questions genuine. Don't be afraid to admit ignorance or helplessness. Ask to be informed, to be helped.

When you ask, use the other person's name. Use your questions to build or reinforce relationships.

2. Listen.

As Stephen Covey says, "Seek first to understand, and then to be understood." The organization that doesn't listen to its customers — internal and external — is headed for trouble.

Three things happen when you listen:

- When you're listening, somebody's talking. Being a good listener is a natural way to get involvement.

- When you're listening, you're learning. Listening keeps you from jumping to false conclusions. Listening lets you collect information for the decisions you have to make.

- When you're listening, you're building or strengthening a relationship. As someone once said, "In some of the best conversations I've ever had, I've hardly said a word."

Recently an executive at another company was sent from headquarters to solve a major customer service problem at a regional office. Almost his first words to the regional office manager were: "My job is to help you do your job. But I can't help you if I don't know what you need. I can't help you if I don't know what your problems are."

Those words were liberating. The office manager had never felt free to state her problems. The few times she had tried, she had found herself in a cycle of shame and blame. But now, feeling that she would be listened to, she was able to identify the sources of the region's problems. And she was able to become part of the solution.

3. Reinforce.

When you've asked the questions, and listened to the answers, then do the right thing with the information you get. Reinforce the positive.

Reinforcing the positive serves two purposes. First, it keeps a good thing going. And second, it recognizes people for the work they have done. So follow Ken Blanchard's advice to "catch people doing things right."

Try these tools. The process of asking, listening, and reinforcing can go a long way toward creating empathy in your organization.

MEETINGS OF THE MINDS

An acquaintance known for his irreverent views once posted a screen-saver on his computer that read,

"Meetings: the practical alternative to work." Practically everyone who read it laughed in understanding acknowledgment. Finally, the poor guy had to change the message because, with so many people stopping and laughing at it, he couldn't get any work done!

Laugh as we might about meetings, they are a necessary part of most organizations' existence. And, to be sure, they can provide valuable benefits. They allow groups or teams to get together and exchange valuable information and ideas "in real time."

> "Treat everyone you meet as if he or she is the most important person you'll meet that day."
> — Roger Dawson, *Secrets of Power Persuasion*

They are a forum for discussion of new directions and a springboard for problem-solving. They can, at times, be the glue that holds teams together — a necessity for communications and cooperative effort. So why do so many of us hate the idea of attending yet another meeting?

It's probably because, improperly managed, meetings can be one of the most insidious time-wasters imaginable. (And it *is* easy to rationalize a lack of work when you've been in a meeting.) Most organizations spend lots of time in meetings. Yet some time management experts have estimated that half the time spent in meetings is wasted.

What's responsible for this wasted time? Participants who either ramble or completely withhold participation. Participants with hidden agendas.

Interruptions. Unproductive conflicts. Unsuitable physical arrangements.

Effective leaders solve these problems before they start. Ask yourself whether your meetings are lean, mean and productive — or a bloated, ineffective waste of time? In case you don't get the answer you're looking for, below are a few suggestions for conducting effective meetings. (I'm still working to improve my performance at holding effective meetings. There seems to be a general consensus in my organization that I talk too much.)

1. Ask, "Is the meeting necessary?"

Many meetings are not worth the time, no matter how brief. The regular staff meeting that "has always been held" and meetings held to spread the accountability for a decision (many times a minor one) very often waste everybody's time.

Ask this question: "Is this meeting worth having?" If the answer is "no," you've saved some time — maybe a lot!

2. Plan the meeting.

A meeting's purpose, with rare exceptions, should be defined clearly and communicated to participants in advance. This is best accomplished by an agenda.

One technique for encouraging a state of readiness among the participants is to put agenda items in question form. For example, instead of the agenda item "Distribution of Assignments on the Chicago Proposal," try "What do you want to be responsible for on the Chicago proposal?"

3. Look closely at who should attend.

Peter Drucker, in his book *The Effective Executive*, refers to one financial executive who routinely asked all his direct subordinates to every meeting, because he feared that uninvited people would feel left out. He decided to cut attendance, yet without slighting the status needs of his subordinates, by using the following printed form:

> "I have asked _____ to meet with me Wednesday at 3, in the fourth floor conference room to discuss _____. Please come if you think that you need the information or want to take part in the discussion. In any event, you will receive a full summary of the discussion and of any decisions made, together with a request for your comments."

Only those needed should attend a meeting. In a case where input is needed from a participant on only one agenda item, that person should be asked to drop in only when this item comes up. Unnecessary attendance at meetings not only wastes the time of the unneeded participants, but also wastes everyone else's time. The larger the group, the more irrelevant questions will be asked, often only for the sake of appearances.

In any case, a great number of participants hinders the establishment of direct communication and makes it more difficult to bring the meeting to closure.

4. Carefully consider the timing of the meeting.

Obviously, it is unproductive to schedule a meeting at a time when key participants can't be available. It may be equally unproductive, however, to schedule the meeting at certain times of the day, even though all necessary persons can attend. For example, a meeting scheduled immediately after lunch often wanders, because participants are often experiencing a lull in their energy level, and because there is less time pressure to end the meeting before quitting time.

Meetings scheduled an hour before lunch or an hour before quitting time are likely to end within a reasonable time. Participants concerned with getting away on time will be more inclined to stick to the main purpose of the meeting.

5. Consider the meeting's location and physical arrangements.

The meeting should be conducted in a place that is adequately comfortable and free of noise and distractions. Needed equipment should be readily available.

If the meeting is for the purpose of problem solving or brainstorming, a circular arrangement is usually more conducive to getting input from all present. If the meeting leader is in a dominant position, such as at the head of a conference table, productive feedback or cross-communication may be discouraged. To encourage discussing, the meeting leader should move from behind his or her desk or away from the head of the conference table.

If, however, a meeting is solely for the purpose of dissemination of information, the leader should place himself or herself in a dominant position, such as behind his or her desk. For sessions requiring the issuance of limited information or brief information exchange, the leader should remain standing. A stand-up meeting keeps people from getting too comfortable or distracted, and it creates a sense of urgency. Consequently, the subjects at hand can be discussed quickly, energetically and effectively — and then the meeting can be adjourned.

6. Start the meeting on time and stick to a strict schedule.

Meeting agendas, of course, always list the time the meeting is to start. However, it is a rare meeting that starts on time. Starting meetings on time, every time, will quickly result in all participants' being on time.

When the starting time for meetings is not taken seriously, each successive meeting tends to get under way later and later. Why? Because there are not sanctions on the many games participants are inclined to play. For example, the participant who consciously or unconsciously is trying to establish a position of importance or power by arriving late has to arrive later and later to be behind all the others. A regular practice of starting meetings on time also quickly gets the message to the "harried executive" who always comes late.

Each item on the meeting agenda should also be timed. This practice encourages the appropriate discussion leader or presenter to come prepared to get to the point and finish on time. In rare cases when an unanticipated twist comes up, the meeting leader can of course allow the discussion to run over the time limit. Setting time limits on each agenda item, however, tends to keep everyone aware of the relative importance of each items and discourages irrelevant discussion, or giving more time to a particular topic than it is worth.

The time-saving benefits to starting meetings on time (at least at first) and to putting estimated times on each agenda item are not always immediate. Poor meeting practices from the past will take a while to go away.

7. Take charge during and after the meeting.

Ensuring that a meeting is effective is as much an art as a skill. The art can be enhanced, however, by following the above suggestions and these few additional pointers:

a. Take necessary action to keep the meeting productive and to-the-point, by redirecting off-the-track discussion, summarizing, testing for consensus, and heading off unproductive conflict or the addition of special-interest items to the agenda.

b. Prevent interruptions by discouraging the practice of coming and going (except for invited presenters on specific points) and by having messages and phone calls screened for later handling by the meeting participants.

c. End the meeting on time — unless an overrun is absolutely necessary. The practice of ending meetings on time allows participants to plan their time after the meeting with greater confidence.

d. See that minutes are promptly prepared and distributed.

e. Follow up to ensure that decisions made in the meeting result in specific assignments with deadlines for completion.

When the above suggestions become regular practice in organizations or departments, time is saved and meetings become more effective. Aside from the obvious benefits, the morale of all participants is enhanced. An increase in morale, with a lowering of frustrations from "too much time wasted in meetings," can have multiple benefits for the organization — perhaps most notably increased cooperation and improved performance.

WORDS FROM WYNCOM

"Regardless of people with whom you work, involving all walks of life and professions, it has been proven to me time and time again how important it is to treat everyone with courtesy and respect with a desire to understand their viewpoint and particular situation. This has been especially true with the many different types of people who have been involved with WYNCOM and the constant deadlines." – *Anna Jarvis*

"Cooperation develops friendships. When I know I'm working with friends, as a team, my performance has to improve." – *Dan Lesher*

"My personal performance improves through cooperation with others. Through cooperation, I have learned to rely on other people to help me with problems. A second opinion is always of help." – *James Hendrix*

"I remember the time I drove up to a hotel and could not recognize it because it was undergoing renovations. We had over 1,100 people coming to a program who needed to get to the ballroom on the bottom level of the hotel. Only one elevator worked and this was a hardhat area. The only way we were able to turn the event into a successful one was through utter teamwork! We had to lead attendees down small narrow maintenance steps, and the wait staff even went to the trouble of serving coffee to attendees who were standing in line to register. The whole day could have been a fiasco; instead, it was one of our most successful programs that year." – *Laurie Shipp*

"I have learned that in most cases, a good idea can be made better by getting others' input. I have had good ideas that when polished and improved by others became great ideas." – *Linda Rogers*

"Listening is much harder than talking. However the more you listen, the more doors you will see opened, which will provide you with unlimited opportunity."
– *Bob Benson*

"I would hope that what people see from me is a positive, friendly, open attitude that says I'm accessible. Your ideas are important to me and will be seriously considered, though not always accepted. Nor would I expect you to accept mine, but seriously consider them in the overall picture. I want people to see an attitude of leadership that builds camaraderie and teamwork. Through building camaraderie and teamwork, we end up with strength that we wouldn't have individually." – *Jerry Miller*

"The style of cooperating that Larry and I share is sometimes seen by the WYNCOM staff as amusing, at the least. And perhaps weird. But you need the talents of people who can think logically, and you need the dreamers. Typically, I take the more management-oriented role, while he's the dreamer, coming up with ideas. He's thinking 10 years down the road, and I'm thinking, 'OK, when does the mail go out, how many printers do we need, how many people must we hire?' I have learned more from Larry than anybody because he forces me to think about things in a different way. And I think I've taught him as well, maybe even to be a little more organized." – *Bunny Holman*

The Communicating Leader

Dealing with change — together

by Kenneth W. Davis

Leadership is about change. Good leaders know how to change other people — and how to change themselves. But good leaders also know when *not* to change. Even more important, they know what to do instead.

To learn when to change and when not to change, consider the words *communication* and *community.* The two words are cousins. Both derive from the Latin word *communis,* meaning "common." But these words have even deeper roots, in the words *ko* and *mei* (pronounced "may"). In Indo-European, ancestor of dozens of languages from Icelandic to English to Sanskrit, *ko* meant "together" and *mei* meant "change."

For English-speakers, the most familiar descendants of *ko* are words beginning with the prefixes *co-, con-,* and *com-,* meaning "together" or "with." To *cooperate,* for example, is to "work together"; to *convene* is to "gather together"; to *converse* is to "take turns with"; and our *companions,* our *company,* are those we "take bread with."

Descendants of *mei,* "change," are less common in English. *Mutate, transmute,* and *migrate* refer to kinds of change, and *mutual* derives from the Latin for "in exchange." From a Greek word for change we get our word *amoeba,* for an ever-changing organism.

Both roots, *ko* and *mei*, led to *communication* and *community*. At root, a community is a group of people who "change together." Communication is what keeps communities together and what lets them change. Good leaders know how — and when — to use communication for these two purposes.

How Organizations Grow

Communities are *like* amoebas — or like any living thing. They have the potential to grow and evolve. This growth and evolution is not necessarily in size; it can be in intelligence, for example, or in flexibility, or in wisdom.

In whatever direction an organization grows, it rarely grows in a straight line. Instead, communities, like children, grow in "spurts," making gains, then pausing to consolidate those gains. And like children, communities have "growing pains," because change is always painful.

One way, then, to picture organizational growth is as a series of steps, or plateaus, with each plateau a consolidation, or recuperation, after the previous rise. But another way is as a spiral, cycling through phases of *ko* and *mei*, of consolidation and change.

In the *mei* phase of each cycle, a leader's job — really, everybody's job — is to promote change, in whatever direction the organization wants to grow. In the *ko* phase of each cycle, a leader's job — and, again, we're *all* leaders — is to bring the organization together. This bringing-together heals the inevitable damage of the last *mei* phase and prepares the organization for the *next mei* phase.

Naturally, these phases aren't always clearly defined, and they can vary from one part of an organization to another. But if you start looking for them, you'll recognize them when they happen.

Questions for Leaders

To be a more effective leader, in whatever arena you're called on to lead, ask yourself these questions:

1. In what direction, if any, is my organization growing? In size? In strength? In intelligence? In wisdom? In what direction does it *want* to grow? In what direction do *I* want it to grow?

2. Is our organization now in a *ko* phase or a *mei* phase, a time of consolidation or a time of change?

3. If we are in a *ko* phase, what togetherness have we achieved so far? What damage caused by the last *mei* phase still needs to be healed? What can *I* do to heal that damage and help our organization become more of a community? When will we be ready for another *mei* phase?

4. If we are in a *mei* phase, what change have we accomplished so far? What change is still possible? What can *I* do to bring about that change? When will we need another *ko* phase?

For further reading . . .

Chappell, Tom. *The Soul of a Business: Managing for Profit and the Common Good* (Bantam). Chapter 4, "Building Community: The Power of Storytelling," is a powerful narrative of the process of going beyond teams to build genuine community at Tom's of Maine.

Covey, Stephen R. *Principle-Centered Leadership* (Summit). Chapter 21, "Involving People in the Problem," discusses the importance of team approaches to change and the problems that result from it.

Covey, Stephen R. *The Seven Habits of Highly Effective People* (Simon & Schuster). Covey's habits 4, 5 and 6 are fundamental tools for cooperation: "Think Win/Win," "Seek First to Understand, Then to Be Understood" and "Synergize."

Deep, Sam, and Lyle Sussman. *Yes, You Can!* (Seminars by Sam Deep). Chapter 4, "Build Relationships," and Chapter 5, "Motivate Others," include a number of helpful lists of specific techniques for achieving greater cooperation in the workplace.

Ends, Earl J., and Curtis W. Page. *Organizational Team Building* (Winthrop). Long before "team" became a buzz word, this 1977 book clearly laid out the key concepts, skills and stages involved in building work teams.

Harper, Bob, and Ann Harper. *Succeeding as a Self-Directed Work Team: Twenty Important Questions Answered* (Harper). This brief, participatory handbook is an effective introduction to introducing and maintaining self-directed teams in the workplace.

Morin, William J. *Trust Me: How to Rebuild Trust in the Workplace* (Harcourt Brace and Company). This book offers a formula for establishing "non-dependent" trust in the workplace, a trust based not on hierarchical relationships, but on open communication between employer and employee.

Peck, M. Scott. *A World Waiting to be Born: Civility Rediscovered* (Bantam). This important book begins with a plea for greater civility in our culture, moves through a discussion of marriage and family, and ends with a specific framework for building and maintaining community in business organizations.

Peters, Tom. *Liberation Management: Necessary Disorganization for the Nanosecond Nineties* (Knopf). While much of this book is concerned with new kinds of workplace cooperation, Chapter 16 discusses self-contained work teams as one of the necessary "basic organizational building blocks."

Peters, Tom. *The Tom Peters Seminar: Crazy Times Call for Crazy Organizations* (Vintage). Chapter 5, "Beyond Disintegration: The Corporation as Rolodex," and Chapter 6, "Beyond Reengineering: Creating a Corporate Talk Show," provide fresh metaphors for how people can work together in new ways.

Sanborn, Mark. *Teambuilt: Making Teamwork Work* (Master Media). In this book, Sanborn presents a six-step process for "making teamwork work": locate, educate, cooperate, communicate, motivate and celebrate.

Senge, Peter M. *The Fifth Discipline: The Art and Practice of the Learning Organization* (Doubleday). Chapter 12 of this book moves beyond the concept of work teams to the concept of "wisdom teams," teams engaged in collective learning. This chapter draws much of its insight from the work of physicist David Bohm, who defined the process of "dialogue."

Waitley, Denis. *Empires of the Mind: Lessons to Lead and Succeed in a Knowledge-Based World* (Morrow). In pages 153-155, Waitley discusses the three best practices of teams at Harris Corporation: "unambiguous, measurable goals, which the leadership constantly reinforces," "a results-driven structure for organizing plans and scheduling and documenting team process" and "team competence, which usually increases when members embody a blend of skills and desire."

Waitley, Denis. *Timing is Everything: Turning Your Seasons of Success into Maximum Opportunities* (Nelson). Chapter 14, "The Season for Establishing Relationships," surveys the three main factors behind "good field morale": delegating, communicating, negotiating.

Webb, MaryLou W., and JoAnn B. Haberer. *TQM: 50 Ways to Make It Work for You* (Crisp Publications). This user-friendly workbook, designed for either individual study or group training, promotes application of the practical interpersonal skills essential to any effective Total Quality Management program.

Wheatley, Margaret J. *Leadership and the New Science: Learning about Organization from an Orderly Universe* (Berrett-Koehler). The principles that Wheatley draws from cutting-edge science can be effectively applied to any organization.

FORGET
WORRY

CHAPTER

6

Y ou probably remember "Don't Worry, Be Happy," Bobby McFerrin's optimistic pop hit from the late 1980s. The catchy tune and lyrics echoed a fantasy shared by many people who dream of casting their cares away. If only it were that easy to achieve such an upbeat state of mind!

Though forgetting worry may not be as simple as the song implies, it is absolutely necessary if we want to do our best work. When beset by worry, we either cope or give in to it. Creativity, and even the ability to think straight, is impossible for someone who is nervous or worried. Fear can act as a physical stimulant by triggering the release of adrenaline, but it actually causes the brain to shut down (with long-term memory being the first to go). You can become so gripped by worry that you are unable to figure out what action to take — which could prevent worrying in the first place.

What is worry, anyway? My definition of worry is anxiety about something over which I have no control, which may not occur, perhaps something I haven't even identified. That is the least useful kind of anxiety there is. As Thomas Jefferson said, "How much pain evils have cost us that have never happened." Of course, before you can stop yourself from worrying, you have to recognize when you're doing it. Some of us are so used to worrying we don't even notice it. We simply fall back on any number of bad habits that might anesthetize the pain of stress

> "Let our advance worrying become advance thinking and planning."
> — Winston Churchill

without eradicating it. Before we know it, our state of worry invites the appearance of all kinds of related demons like depression, sleeplessness, anger, procrastination and lowered self-esteem.

The first step I take to forget worry and avoid its inhibiting side effects is to identify exactly what I'm worried about. It's amazing how frequently we just don't stop to figure out what's bothering us, and don't consider whether we can take action to alleviate our distress.

Often, worry is caused by fear of taking a risk and possibly making a mistake or even failing entirely. Whether consciously or not, we torment ourselves with questions like, "Will I be embarrassed in front of my peers, lose my job, go bankrupt?" Risk-taking phobia, a major impediment to creativity, is rooted in insecurity based on the training we receive from an early age to give the "right" answer. In truth, there can be many "right" answers based on any number of variables involved in a situation. It all depends on how open our minds are to creative thinking, which is directly dependent on the degree of worry involved.

The source of worry is not always obvious, and identifying it can take some patience and persistence. Worry might even stem from multiple or overlapping sources. One method I use to push past fear is to jot down a brief "worst case" scenario, as suggested in *Conceptual Blockbusting* by James L. Adams. In this scenario, I detail exactly what would happen to me if everything went wrong. Am I concerned about the possibility of jeopardizing my reputation, an important business deal, my health? By making these points specific and then facing them, I swap my ability to analyze with my fear of failure — a highly effective trade-off.

Once I understand the cause of my worry, I ask myself, "What, if anything, can I do to resolve this situation?" At this stage, I can determine whether there is any action, or any number of actions, I can take. As soon as I have removed worry from the picture, my mental myopia improves. It is usually generalities and stereotypes that prompt worry and prevent us from thinking about what we perceive to be true. Free of worry, I can see things from different points of view and generate new beliefs about them.

WORRY-FREE CHOICES

There are many choices to make when you are ready to get back in control and forget worry. I'm sure there are options, perhaps unique, that work for you. You might want to select from this menu of actions that I've found effective (I often go for a combination platter):

- Reassure yourself that this situation is part of life and should have no long-term effect on your sense of confidence or worth.

- Think of how someone you admire and trust would handle the situation. Whenever possible, discuss it with this person. (I usually turn to my business partner and wife, Bunny, for guidance.)

- Substitute the concept of "challenge," "opportunity" or "lesson" for "worry."

- Find and appreciate the humorous aspect(s) of the situation.

- Seek further details that might reveal a solution faster or prove there is actually nothing to worry about.

- Delegate the problem to someone who may be in a better position to handle it.

- At an appropriate time and place, vent your feelings to people who are likely to understand and be able to help.

- Sleep on it. The situation could look different after you take time out, get some rest and then approach it from a fresh perspective.

If it turns out there is nothing I can do about a situation, I ultimately shift my attention somewhere else. I have learned that to keep worrying about something I can't change gets me nowhere.

LIVING REALISTICALLY BUT POSITIVELY IN THE PRESENT

In the business world, anyone is vulnerable to worry, even people who enjoy their careers and know they are well qualified for their positions. You might feel uncomfortable or out of sorts when not in your workplace. You might fall into the habit of getting to work early and going home late, without necessarily ac-

> "We are, perhaps, uniquely among the earth's creatures, the worrying animal. We worry away our lives, fearing the future, discontent with the present, unable to take in the idea of dying, unable to sit still."
> — Lewis Thomas

complishing more than your associates who keep regular hours. You might find yourself distracted by thoughts of work even in social situations with family or friends.

These common kinds of work-related worry usually occur when people don't live in the present. Our physical selves live in the present, but that doesn't mean our minds do. Our minds can travel from the present to the future or the past in an instant. If we implement this incredible human ability to our benefit, we can look forward to the good times that lie ahead or enjoy memories of wonderful moments we've had.

To one extent or another, though, many of us tend to think about the future or contemplate the past in a negative context. We are distracted by thoughts of what we need to do later in the day or week. We find it hard to loosen our mental grip on difficult circumstances and people who have made us miserable. While it's certainly important to plan ahead as well as learn from previous experiences, the inability or refusal to live each moment as it happens makes people feel overwhelmed by life, and they are out of control.

I have discovered that the more I accept whatever is going on "now," the better able I am to turn that moment to my advantage. When I truly live in the present, I notice how much more in control I feel and, therefore, how much freer I am to think and act creatively. Goal-setting is essential for success, of course, but we must give ourselves the opportunity to reach our goals instead of being manipulated by them.

Realism is also a vital factor in setting goals that don't inflict worry. If you aren't tall you won't ever be the center on your basketball team, no matter how deep your desire or intense your hours of practice — but you might become an NBA player like 5-foot-3 Mugsy Bogues, starting point guard with the Charlotte Hornets. Why waste time trying to achieve the impossible when there is so much that you *can* accomplish?

It's a common belief that worry stems from the pace of life today. From early morning, people are faced with a day full of deadlines, demands and problems. In the evening, they pick up the kids, rush home, make dinner, do paper work. The sheer number of these activities is enough to make any mere mortal quake, right? No, not really. Rather than being the result of having too much to do, worry arises from a perspective that's too negative. In their book *Yes, You Can!* Sam Deep and Lyle Sussman suggest that people would do well to change the way they foresee events that appear to be overwhelming. "Convince yourself there's something good in it," they advise, "and look forward to those benefits."

True workaholics enjoy working, and they choose to do so without fear that the other parts of their lives are suffering as a result. I'm not suggesting that their personal lives *won't* suffer, but they won't worry about it. All the hours they put in won't afflict *them* with ulcers, nervous

> "Consider the stress feelings you may have about your dreams. Your dreams should be big enough to stretch you but not stress you. Don't attach worrisome obligations to your life as you dream. Forge your dreams in such a way that you dream them stress-FREE. If you feel clenching pangs of tightness as you dream, consider dreaming a different dream!"
> — Denis Waitley, *Timing is Everything*

breakdowns or high blood pressure (although their neglected and worried family members might fall victim to such problems).

It's the pseudo-workaholics — those who think they *should* be working although they don't really want to, who work extra hours because of pressures other than self-satisfaction — who are in danger of stress-induced illnesses.

These people may be beleaguered by lack of cooperation and trust among their colleagues, or an autocratic boss who values only his or her own ideas. Even if unpleasant conditions like these exist in the workplace, people must learn to cope with them or find ways to change them. Worry won't make their problems disappear. (Incidentally, Chapter 11 of this book may be helpful to those workaholics and pseudo-workaholics whose family lives are suffering.)

A PSYCHOSOMATIC 'CURE' FOR STRESS

If stress-related ailments are psychosomatic, the "cure" must incorporate psychological as well as physical adaptations. Obviously, adopting an emotionally healthy approach to life cannot repair a malfunctioning heart or erase other permanent damage to the body. But it can help people learn new ways of coping with worry that do not mean making a choice between living a long life and living a happy one.

From my earlier days as a basketball player, I have seen time and again that my physical condition is profoundly affected by my mental attitude, and vice versa. No sooner do I allow myself to ease off exercise and start to get out of shape than my levels of optimism and energy begin to wane, as well. You don't have to become obsessed with exercise or subscribe to the theory of "no pain, no gain." Just devise a routine of regular aerobic activity, under the guidance of a doctor or physical trainer, that will keep you healthy, energetic and productive. We have an exercise room at WYNCOM that employees are encouraged to use whenever it is convenient for them. Hopping on a treadmill, riding the stationary bike or using free weights followed by a sauna are painless ways to tone muscles while clearing cobwebs from a worried mind.

Diet is also directly related to our mental and physical well-being. It seems the very things people crave when they're worried — sweets and alcohol — actually exacerbate anxiety. Next time you're ready to grab a candy bar to lift your spirits, reach

> "Finish each day and be done with it . . . you have done what you could; some blunders and absurdities no doubt crept in; forget them as soon as you can. Tomorrow is a new day; you shall begin it well and serenely."
> — Ralph Waldo Emerson

for an apple instead. You may be surprised how altering your eating and drinking habits can have a positive effect on your outlook as well as your shape.

Another effective way to bolster your spirits and physique simultaneously is to practice some kind of relaxation or meditation techniques. It doesn't matter whether you follow a formal, step-by-step program or simply take time to listen to soothing music. You may want to try diaphragmatic breathing or biofeedback. Whatever method you prefer, relax once a day, however briefly, when you're not rushed or pressured. That day either becomes much easier to get through or looks better in retrospect.

Active relaxation (known in some circles as "play") is helpful, too, as the WYNCOM writing team can attest. To shed the anxieties that can accompany the solitary work of writing on deadline, the team sometimes sets aside 20 minutes for an invigorating session at the neighborhood laser-tag site. Dressed in black for optimal camouflage, the writers strap on space-age weaponry and zap each other with beams of light. Emerging from the group workout laughing and out of breath, they are armed with a refreshed perspective that allows them to return to their assignments with new vigor and greater creativity.

It's important to keep in mind that relaxation, whether active or passive, is not a reflexive response. It is an activity that is learned through repetition and works best when practiced at a time that is free from strain, rather than in the midst of tension. Trying to relax while under pressure usually only increases frustration, because the body obstinately refuses to offer relief when it's producing adrenaline.

COEXISTING COMFORTABLY WITH RISK

Perhaps no other society in history has been so aware of the dangers that exist in the world. We are warned daily about threats of overpopulation, deterioration of the ozone layer, toxic substances running amok. On top of these universal concerns are the more personalized ones that plague us in relation to careers, family, health and finances.

The litany of worries we face can seem endless and make us feel paralyzed. Yet life without risk would be so mundane that there would be little motivation to think, be creative and take action. When you realize that trouble can hide around any corner (from the perils of a slippery bathtub to a drunk driver), it becomes clear how pointless and obstructive it is to worry about things we either can't identify or can't change.

Once we understand how to use information, common sense and a little help from our friends to define our fears, seek solutions and take action, we will be capable of forgetting worry and becoming more productive, better balanced, healthier and, yes, happier individuals.

Words from WYNCOM

"I just refuse to worry excessively. I reached a point where I realized that life was too short and too precious to bother with worry and guilt. If I can choose, and I almost always can, I'll be positive rather than negative. I try to make the best decisions I can with the information I have at the time, and learn from the results. It really helps to be with a company where you're not penalized for making an honest mistake." – *Elaine Rutherford*

"I just set my mind to what needs to be done. If you dwell on it without working on it, you're much less productive. If I'm away from the office and can't work on the problem at the time, I find something else to do – usually a physical task. For me, that often means working in the yard." – *Susan Thacker*

"I don't worry about things I can't change. I do the best I can with what I have. I get past worry by making a continuous effort toward what I need and want to do. Away from the office, I make a mental note on what I need to do when I get there, and then I follow through by doing whatever is necessary to solve the problem."
– *Sheila Hardaway*

"If I'm at home, I tell myself, 'This is my home time. I'm not going to worry.' It's taken a long time to develop that self-discipline. Worrying will drag you down."
– *Barbra Renkey*

"Think the problem through, or talk it out with someone. Having a sounding board is helpful." – *Paula Boycott*

"I use humor. If I can get away from the problem and laugh about it for just a minute, I find I can then look at the problem and deal with it in a different light."
— *Becky Dean*

"I make a list, prioritize the items, and follow it to the letter. Seeing it written down makes it seem less imposing, and it gives me an agenda." — *Karen Langdon*

"Dealing with worry or stress is a matter of perspective — keeping the bigger picture in mind. When I lived in California, I would go out after work each day and look at the ocean. That put things in perspective for me. I'm new at my job with WYNCOM, but rather than worrying about being new, I'm trying to act as a sponge, just learning everything I can." — *Bob Benson*

Please don't take it personally

by Jeff Walter

Even people in empowered organizations sometimes get their feelings hurt, say **Sam Deep** and **Lyle Sussman**, co-authors of the books *Smart Moves* and *What to Say to Get What You Want*. But good communication skills can help solve, or even prevent, these kinds of problems — giving team members fewer things to worry about.

Deep, an organizational consultant and trainer based in the Pittsburgh area, and Sussman, professor of management at the University of Louisville, recently discussed ways a growing company can stay healthy and productive as it moves away from traditional management practices and toward a culture of shared leadership.

"As teams become more empowered, the tendency to be hurt increases. That is the cost of teamwork," Sussman said. He added that, as the top-down hierarchies and rigid job descriptions of the traditional organization disappear, the importance of communication is greater than ever.

As employees try to adapt to their new, ever-changing roles and responsibilities in an empowered workforce, it is perhaps inevitable that misunderstandings will arise. One of the keys to continued success and happiness is remaining focused on the bigger picture and not getting caught up in petty differences or perceived slights.

Deep offered three memorable quotations that can help us keep our minds on what's important while ignoring the "small-minded stuff."

- "Never attribute to malice that which can be explained by incompetence."

- "Give people credit for their stupidity."

- "When the elephants fight, it's the grass that suffers."

The last quotation, an African proverb, points out the destructiveness that feuds and infighting can wreak within an organization. The other two remind us that, in most cases, when people hurt us, it is not intentional. And that means we shouldn't waste our time worrying about it.

"I'll never forget one time when I was working in an engineering company," Deep said. "The engineers were complaining: 'Those people in top management are trying to do it to us . . . they're just making life difficult for us. They're *conspiring* against us.'

"I went to the vice presidents — there were 11 of them in this company — and said, 'Let me tell you what the engineers are saying.' When I told them, those vice presidents laughed. They said, 'We wish we had the *ability* to conspire in such a way!' "

Sussman added: "I think a lot of people walk around feeling victimized. Their knee-jerk reaction is that the other person *meant* to do it. And you play that scenario out: The person woke up early and laid out a strategic plan to hurt you. If you take this to its ultimate conclusion, it says more about you than it does about the other person, who probably is amazed that you were hurt at all."

Good communication is the best antidote to hurtful situations. Sussman and Deep offered these tips:

1. Understand what's happening. Be open. The very best communicators are good listeners.

2. Know your audience. Knowing people tells you how to communicate with them.

3. Be aware of non-verbal communication. A large part of meaning is derived not from what is said but from factors like tone of voice, eye contact and body language.

Are you a *winner* or a *whiner*?

by Sam Deep and Lyle Sussman

Do you realize that everything you say indicates whether you're a winner or a whiner?

Whether planned or spontaneous, your choice of words, phrasing and tone tells the world who you are. The language you use speaks volumes about your personality, your attitude and your potential for success. It determines not only how other people react to you, but also how you feel about yourself. And, like a stone tossed into a pond, what you say — and the way you say it — has a ripple effect on your entire organization.

From an individual standpoint as well as an organizational one, what you see in your mind is what you create; what you think about is what you get; and what you speak is what you become. Consider this as "The Language of *Whiners* vs. The Language of *Winners.*"

To be a winner, you need a high-powered mental diet that pumps up your resistance to pessimistic thoughts and conversation. Here's a sample menu of a "breakfast of champions":

- Whiners say, "I'll try" but actually mean "I feel compelled to do it, but I really don't want to and I don't expect to succeed." A "try" is nothing more than that. Winners prefer the affirmative "I will."

- When asked how you feel (even rhetorically), say "great" or "marvelous," not just "fine" or "OK." A winner's response makes everyone feel better — including oneself.

- Never say, "I'm too (stupid, fat, short, inexperienced, weak, afraid, disorganized)" to do something. Winners reject these and other negative characterizations.

- Refuse to say or think, "I failed." You might learn a new way not to do something, but you'll never fail.

- By replacing "I can't," "I don't," or "I won't" with "I haven't up until now," you open up a future of endless possibilities instead of slamming doors shut.

- Use the positive language of "It'll be a challenge" instead of the defeatist "It can't be done." History is full of individual and corporate winners who achieved what others said couldn't be done.

- Whiners implore, "Let somebody else deal with it." Winners believe, "Here's my chance to shine."

- An organization can replace whiners' thinking of "We're not as good as . . . " with the winners' conviction of "We're as good as we think we are."

Positive self-talk builds mental fitness and reduces worry by giving you the courage and the energy to get past adversity and explore your potential to the limit. Once you recognize your personal speech patterns, you can identify yourself as a whiner or a winner (and you may be surprised to learn who you really are!). With this new awareness, you'll be able to use the power of positive "self-talk" to improve your mental fitness on a daily basis — and become, or remain, a winner.

For further reading . . .

Adams, James L. *Conceptual Blockbusting: A Guide to Better Ideas* (Addison Wesley). This classic guide to creativity, now in its third edition, gives practical advice for getting past worry and other emotional blocks to good thinking.

Benson, Herbert., with Miriam Z. Klipper. *The Relaxation Response* (Avon). This book provides simple instructions for a scientifically proven meditation technique.

Borysenko, Joan. *Fire in the Soul: A New Psychology of Spiritual Optimism* (Warner). This book makes a persuasive case that we can choose to respond to the inevitable difficulties of life with either fear or love.

Bramson, Robert M. *Coping with Difficult People* (Doubleday). Bramson inventories seven familiar species of difficult people and suggests strategies for coping with each.

Breton, Sue. *Why Worry? How to Stop Worrying and Enjoy Your Life* (Element). Particularly useful in this book is its exploration of varying personality types, how each responds to worry and how each can overcome it.

Covey, Stephen R. *The Seven Habits of Highly Effective People* (Simon & Schuster). Habit 1, "Be Proactive: Principles of Personal Vision," and Habit 7, "Sharpen the Saw," both provide a solid foundation for living with less worry.

Deep, Sam, and Lyle Sussman. *Yes, You Can!* (Seminars by Sam Deep). Chapter 1, "Think Positively," includes lists of helpful pointers toward such outcomes as "increase your self-esteem," "feel more optimistic," "look to the future, forget the past," "forgive your mistakes" and "reduce your worry."

Emery, Gary, and Pat Emery. *The Second Force: Redirecting Your Resistance to Success* (Dutton). This thorough but straightforward guide is based on two principles: "You can choose your thoughts" and "You can create your state of mind."

Hanson, Peter G. *The Joy of Stress: How to Make Stress Work for You* (Andrews, McMeel and Parker). This entertaining book can help you identify and change the usual ways you react to stress.

Harris, Thomas A. *I'm OK—You're OK* (Avon). This classic introduction to transactional analysis provides a simple, elegant framework for understanding and transforming difficult relationships.

Laudan, Larry. *The Book of Risks: Fascinating Facts about the Chances We Take Every Day* (Wiley). On one hand, this book is a worrywart's nightmare, a list of thousands of things that *can* go wrong. But on the other hand, it can be refreshing to learn how unlikely most of these things are. (For example, your chances of dying this year from *any* animal's bite — including snakes and insects — is one in 21 million.)

Mardus, Craig B. *How to Make Worry Work for You: Simple and Practical Lessons on How to Be Happy* (Warner). This scientifically rooted book provides "short-cuts for normal nuts," ways for all of us to rechannel, toward more positive ends, the energy that we often apply to worry.

Moore, Thomas. *Care of the Soul: A Guide for Cultivating Depth and Sacredness in Everyday Life* (Harper Collins). This important book challenges all of us to overcome obstacles of worry, jealousy and depression, by nurturing our inner selves.

Peters, Tom. *The Pursuit of WOW! Every Person's Guide to Topsy-Turvy Times* (Vintage). Virtually every page of this book contains specific tips for "having a little fun" while "making a little money."

Sinetar, Marsha. *Do What You Love, the Money Will Follow* (Dell). This book is an inspiring guide to overcoming the

"Monday morning blues" and finding ways to express your true self in the workplace.

Waitley, Denis. *Empires of the Mind: Lessons to Lead and Succeed in a Knowledge-Based World* (Morrow). Chapter 12, "Self-Leadership and Resilience: Misfortune's Master," is packed with good advice on responding to difficulties with grace and humor.

Waitley, Denis. *Timing is Everything: Turning Your Seasons of Success into Maximum Opportunities* (Nelson). Chapter 15, "The Season for Optimism," offers lists of specific worry-reducing behaviors, including instructions for creating your own personal motivational tape.

THINK
EFFECTIVELY

CHAPTER

W hatever it takes."

Everyone who does business with WYNCOM benefits from the "W.I.T." philosophy made known throughout the company by employee Dennis Deppisch.

Dennis used the phrase to describe a method of thinking that seeks improvement through "general ingenuity and the willingness to do whatever you're asked to further the relationship with the customers or the betterment of the company as a whole."

In a nanosecond, Dennis defined effective thinking.

Thinking effectively, as Dennis knew, is the basic building block of good business. Thinking is something we all do, the basis of what makes us human. From making selections at the grocery store to planning a career, we spend our lives thinking about things, whether trivial or important, that affect us at home and at work. We don't always realize, though, that there are ways of thinking that can help us get to the heart of the matter to make decisions that really work for us and those around us.

It has been said about one of the world's greatest thinkers, "Thomas Edison could do more productive thinking in a single day than many people actually do in a lifetime!" Of course, Edison was a genius, but the emphasis he placed on the impact of creative thinking helped his genius flourish.

I'm not suggesting that society would be better off if we all were clones of Edison. But it couldn't hurt to examine the inventor's methods and consider how they could be applied to our own lives. Edison resolved never to lose the intense, nearly childlike curiosity that enabled him to look at everyday things as if he were seeing them for the first time, without prejudice or stereotype. So often do the rest of us give in to the pressure to be like "everyone else" that we resist the flow of creativity.

This tendency usually begins as we enter grade school, where conformity is encouraged. This is not to discredit the educational system, which obviously has many more pluses than minuses. But most of us can remember an elementary school teacher who put gold stars on the work of children who colored within the lines, but glued no stars on the papers of children who colored outside the lines. As we grow older, conformity is often reinforced by our friends and business associates. How many of us remember suggesting a new idea, only to hear a friend say, "Well, that's a good idea, but . . . " and then proceed to mercilessly, though politely, kill the idea. J. Paul Getty said it well: "No one can possibly achieve any real and lasting success or 'get rich' in business by being a conformist."

Wait a minute, now. I may hear some grumbling from the stands about how life today is incredibly more complex than it was in Edison's time. How can individuals be expected to dream up solutions comparable to the invention of the light bulb? Even if that's true, we can still become much more effective at solving daily problems by gaining access to our creative capabilities.

Now, more than ever, in our knowledge-based world, it is imperative that we become innovative and effective thinkers who flex our mental muscles to solve problems that may never have existed before. P.R. Nayak and J. M. Ketteringham observe in *Breakthroughs!* that innovations don't arise from a rational analysis of the marketplace as much as from "the curiosity of an individual." People who become adept at this kind of thinking, and then put their thoughts into action, will never be out of work.

> "There is one thing stronger than all the armies of the world: and that is an idea whose time has come."
> — Victor Hugo

The initial step in effective thinking is to recognize the tremendous breadth of our mental powers. Here is how Denis Waitley describes the brain: "If we put hundreds of the world's highest-powered computers linked in tandem inside the Empire State Building, we still wouldn't begin to match the information processing ability of one 10-year-old human brain — because your brain is a Xerox machine, a Polaroid camera, a Kodak carousel, a Beta Max video tape recorder, a Technicolor wide screen projector – and billions of miniature microfilm cartridges all delicately designed into one system – all floating in an electro-chemical solution that continues to defy the most sophisticated attempts at duplication."

Most of us do not even begin to use one iota of this astounding capacity because we can't imagine ourselves possessing potential similar to that of inventors, writers, artists or composers. If we accomplish step one and realize the magnitude of our abilities, we then leap to step two: problem perception. How do we view our problems?

> "Most of our so-called reason consists of finding reasons to go on believing as we already do."
> — J.H. Robinson,
> quoted in *Brain Power,* by Karl Albrecht

Do they seem like unwanted headaches or like opportunities for challenge and growth? People like Dennis Deppisch understand that life is a process in which we must constantly solve problems. These are the people who discover the excitement and rewards that exist in even superficially mundane tasks. They tend to be noticeably more creative in their jobs and their personal lives.

Anna Jarvis, Vice President of Operations and Administration, tells this story describing Dennis's thinking style: "Dennis came to WYNCOM about a month after I came on board in January of 1994. From the beginning we worked together to identify several needs within the company. One of the first projects that he worked on was a detailed time line used for tracking the stages of our marketing letters from conception to actual delivery to potential participants. He came up with a system to determine the amount of time required for each stage of the process in order to meet our deadlines. No one had thought of that before."

Before joining WYNCOM, Dennis was manager of computer and technical development for the cable services division of American Express. He also worked in marketing at Lightpath, a high-tech computer digital mapping and software database company. Although Dennis had different responsibilities at WYNCOM, he was successful because he was always ready to apply his thought processes outside his comfort zone or area of direct expertise. Anna sums it up like this: "Regardless of the task at hand, be it setting up a work station, moving furniture, taking a registration or securing sites for the teleconference, Dennis was there."

> "When we speak of *improving the mind* we are usually referring to the acquisition of information or knowledge, or to the *type* of thoughts one *should* have, and not to the actual *functioning* of the mind. We spend little time monitoring our own thinking and comparing it with a more sophisticated ideal."
> — James L. Adams, *Conceptual Blockbusting*

Dennis was with the company for only about 18 months before his untimely death from cancer. His influence, particularly because of his innovative thinking and enthusiasm in all endeavors, has provided lasting impact on the people and processes of the company. His "Whatever It Takes" philosophy continues to be a cornerstone for WYNCOM.

What made this man such an innovative and effective thinker? Essentially, the same things that can make anyone an innovative and effective thinker. While there may be many common traits, I would like to share my observations on the characteristics of an individual with positive thinking skills.

THE EFFECTIVE THINKER:

- **Views problems as opportunities.** Effective thinkers are hungry for challenges that will put their thinking skills to the test. They realize that problems very often lead to great discoveries.

- **Has an appetite for ambiguity.** Few things, and few people, fit into the tidy little boxes we often try to fit them into. It's a complex world with few easy answers. Effective thinkers don't let this bother them. They are ready to adapt to almost any situation.

- **Is self-critical and learns from mistakes.** By "self-critical," I don't mean negative, or paralyzed by perfectionism. I mean simply that effective thinkers expect the best from themselves — and when they don't perform at their best, they find out why, so they can make improvements.

- **Exercises creativity.** Effective thinkers know that creativity is a tool that anyone can learn to use to improve their capacity for problem-solving, innovation and getting things done.

- **Seeks and accepts input from others.** Some people find it difficult, for one reason or another, to ask for help. Not so with effective thinkers. They realize they don't know all the answers and eagerly pursue the synergistic effects made possible through diverse contributions.

- **Recognizes multiple possibilities.** There is generally more than one right answer, more than one solution to the problem. Effective thinkers don't stop at the first idea they come to. They know that their might be another, even better one around the corner.

- **Nurtures curiosity.** Curiosity can be defined as a thirst for knowledge. Effective thinkers are like sponges, soaking up knowledge from diverse sources. They never stop learning, and because of this, they often make effective teachers, eager to share what they've learned.

- **Revises goals when necessary.** Things change. Goals that are set in stone can be deadly. Effective thinkers realize that what worked yesterday won't necessarily work today; they are ready to correct their course as needed.

- **Checks for accuracy and accepts accountability.** No passing the buck here. Effective thinkers accept responsibility, and they put their mental skills to use in visualizing both the big picture and the details, the forest and the trees.

- **Keeps eye on both the short term and the long term.** As a member of the WYNCOM team, Dennis Deppisch was well acquainted with deadlines, so his short-term vision was sharp. But he also realized the importance of the longer view. A deeply spiritual man, Dennis realized the importance of living a balanced life and of leaving a legacy for his family and loved ones. Effective thinkers know there's more to success than the short-term bottom line.

- **Truly enjoys thinking!** Enough said.

There is no truth to the rumor that these attributes are limited to only the lucky few. They are habits that can be acquired and practiced by anyone willing, eager and persistent enough to learn them. It is from the development of these effective thinking strategies that self-leadership emerges.

But the innovative thinker is not the only winner. Organizations prize this kind of self-leadership for the contagious excitement and real benefits it generates for both the individual and the company as a whole, as has been demonstrated at WYNCOM time and again.

HOW WYNCOM ENCOURAGES EFFECTIVE THINKING

1. **A fluid environment.** WYNCOM strives to keep its organizational structure flat. Almost without exception, there are no job titles that separate people into rigid categories of manager, supervisor and worker. This allows people the freedom to creatively float ideas without fear of overstepping their bounds, looking foolish or suffering consequences.

2. **Tolerance for "failure."** As I mentioned earlier in the book, risk taking and experimentation must be accepted as a natural part of the company's growth. Honest mistakes made in pursuit of innovation or superior customer service are different from the "avoidance" types of failure that stifle effective thinking. I have on several occasions made the comment, tongue only partly in cheek, that if someone should happen to bankrupt the company through a well-intentioned effort, I would just respond by saying, "No problem. At least we had fun while it lasted."

3. **Encouragement of team efforts.** Common goals are set, individuals put in ideas, and a group effort puts the best ideas into action. Many teams are not permanent, but ad-hoc collections of people whose complementary skills fit the task at hand.

4. **Shared information.** WYNCOM employees not only attend Lessons in Leadership programs by our speakers, but also have the opportunity to attend seminars and presentations in other areas of professional development.

5. **Opportunities for expressing ideas.** *Drivin' Home*, our weekly in-house newsletter, welcomes input from all employees who want to share news and views with other members of the organization.

These are but a few of the techniques developed through the collective intelligence at WYNCOM. The important thing to keep in mind is that complex problems seldom have simple answers. Understanding and implementing the art of effective thinking will provide fresh insights and solve problems for both individuals and organizations. As Dennis Deppisch was fond of saying, "Whatever It Takes."

WORDS FROM WYNCOM

"People who are effective thinkers come up with ideas based on the reality of the given situation. They look at it from many angles. I try to consistently use a good thought process. I try to listen, ask questions and understand the answers I receive. It's important to tap into people's minds, figure out where they're coming from, and understand the variables — such as peers, family, work and their social and political environments — that have brought them to this point in their lives."
— *Bob Benson*

"When I have a decision to make, I ask: 'Who is this going to affect? How will it help or hurt them? How will it affect me?' It's very important to weigh the consequences of your decision. I think a lot of people get themselves into trouble when they don't think ahead. My husband and I own a house that we converted into apartments. We recently had to make a decision about siding for the house. Our first thought was go ahead with the siding, until we looked at the financial effect for the longer term. By looking at the outcome, we made a good decision to delay having the work done."
— *Sheila Hardaway*

"I think effectively by making sure I have time to do things. Sometimes I have to hope they all fit into the time I have set aside for them, but planning the day in advance really helps. I use commuting time to think about what's ahead for the day. When I'm getting ready to travel to a program, I'll spend some time in the office taking care of details. Then when I'm on the road at a program, and a problem comes up, I'm better able to adjust and solve the problem, because I have taken care of detail work in advance. I know that has helped me in solving last-minute ticket or registration problems with customers who attend our programs." – *Becky Dean*

"Everyone knows his or her own job, but by learning about the jobs of others, you can see the bigger picture – the goals of the company. I have gained a better understanding of my job by talking with the people my work affects. My first week on the job, I answered phone calls, and that helped me understand the process that leads to my work as a registration coordinator."

– *Karen Langdon*

Stephen Covey talks about effectiveness

As author of *The 7 Habits of Highly Effective People*, Dr. Stephen Covey is considered something of an authority on effectiveness. WYNCOM is fortunate to have a close working relationship with Dr. Covey, and I recently sat down with him and "picked his brain" on the subject.

Larry Holman: How would you define effectiveness?

Stephen Covey: I would say that effectiveness is getting results — and that it means that you *continue* to get results. You're not effective if you just get what you want now, and kill the goose that lays the golden eggs, that keeps on producing the results. So if you get what you want out of a relationship, and also nurture the quality of that relationship so it continues to produce good things, I would say the combination is effectiveness.

LH: But it's possible to achieve many goals without being effective.

SC: I think you have to decide: What are the results that you want? Many people climb the ladder of success that the world has essentially programmed them into, and they get one rung after another, and then they get to the top of that ladder of success because they've accomplished all their goals. Then they discover it's leaning against the wrong wall. They didn't deal with the question of "Wait a minute, what is it we're *really* about? What *are* the desired results we really want?" So effectiveness means you have to decide what are those desired results. They should be *worthy* desired results. They should be transcendentally *important* desired results. And you should keep them coming over time.

So those are three elements: the definition of what the desired results are, so that you make sure they're worthy and balanced and whole, and then the *getting* of them, and then the preserving of the goose so that you *keep on* getting them on a regular basis.

LH: What is the difference between effectiveness and mere efficiency?

SC: I'd say that efficiency deals more with things, and effectiveness with people. Efficiency is more of a *management* concept, and effectiveness is more of a *leadership* concept. Efficiency deals more with speed, effectiveness more with direction and destination.

Both are important. I think the leadership issue — of deciding what the right job is, deciding what wall to put the ladder against, deciding what those desired results are — comes first. Then, once you've got a relationship among the people who are working on that, so that they're all committed to that vision, you've got effectiveness. Now, go for efficiency. Climb that ladder as fast as you possibly can. Now manage; now control. Let people manage themselves, really, because they're really being directed by the common vision that they settled on, which dealt with effectiveness or leadership.

LH: Peter Drucker's 1967 book, *The Effective Executive*, is considered one of the classic pieces of literature on the subject of effectiveness. Drucker says

**executives are expected to get the right things done —
or, more simply, to be effective.**

SC: Another statement by Peter Drucker is that
"effectiveness cannot be taught, but it must be learned." In
other words, you cannot give to another, really, what
effectiveness is, and turn them into an effective person.
They have to exercise their own gifts and endowments and
talents to act on the basis of the principles of effectiveness
to really learn what effectiveness is.

He also said that "plans are worthless, but planning is
invaluable." Well, why would he say that? Because
planning — the activity of thinking ahead, of anticipating —
really is one of the aspects of true effectiveness. But what
you come up with might have to change constantly because
of changing circumstances. You have to keep coming up
with them. Unless you update your five-year plan annually.

**LH: In your book *First Things First*, you applied
the principles of *The 7 Habits of Highly Effective People*
to daily problems of life. You said that effectiveness
begins when the "first things" are identified.**

SC: "First things first," in relation to effectiveness,
would mean you have to first decide what the first things
are. What is the wall you want to lean your ladder against?
What are the most important things? Then, once you decide
that, you've made the decision of leadership. Now, manage
yourself in a way that you go after those first things by
putting them first. That's management, see. So leadership
preceded management, and effectiveness preceded
efficiency. Now, if you do it in a way that also preserves
the ability to keep producing that, now you've got the real

essence of effectiveness, because the goose keeps laying those golden eggs.

LH: What's the difference between the effective person and the ineffective person? Are there any signs?

SC: I would say the telltale signs of an ineffective person would be that their successes don't last, are temporary and fleeting and ephemeral. And their lives are not balanced. They may have so-called success in one part of their life, but their personal life or family life may be in shambles. And so they don't have a sense of wisdom and proportion and balance among all of the dimensions of their life.

LH: Can a person be efficient but ineffective?

SC: The statement is often made that many people go about their jobs efficiently ineffective. In other words, they're climbing that ladder quickly and efficiently, but it's leaning against the wrong wall. They're selling a lot, but there's buyer's regrets next month. They got their kids to cooperate and clean the house, but when they're on a trip the kids won't do anything. They essentially are quick about their actions, but they're just simply going the wrong direction. Another way of putting it is: To double your speed in the wrong direction is doubly efficient but doubly ineffective at the same time.

Nearly three decades later, Drucker book is still effective

An effective executive doesn't just do things right — he or she also must have the ability to "get the right things done." So says Peter Drucker in his 1967 classic of management literature, *The Effective Executive* (HarperCollins, New York).

According to Drucker, who's widely considered the father of management, the need for effectiveness stems from the increasing numbers of knowledge workers, as opposed to manual workers. An "executive" is any knowledge worker who materially contributes to an organization's capacity to perform and obtain results. And it's an executive's job to be effective.

Effectiveness *must* be learned because our range of abilities and resources is limited; our best hope is to make better use of what we have. In Drucker's words:

"If one cannot increase the supply of a resource, one must increase its yield. And effectiveness is the one tool to make the resources of ability and knowledge yield more and better results.

"Effectiveness thus deserves high priority because of the needs of an organization. It deserves even greater priority as the tool of the executive and as his access to achievement and performance."

The author sees effectiveness as a habit, or a complex of learnable practices, as opposed to a personality trait. That means *all* of us can learn effectiveness.

The five essential practices for business effectiveness, as defined by Drucker, are:

- Effective knowledge and management of time.
- Focus on outward contribution, or results.
- Ability to optimize strengths.
- Setting the right priorities.
- Making effective decisions.

Throughout the book, Drucker spells out what is needed to become effective in each of the above areas. Effective time management, for example, is a three-step process: recording time, managing time and consolidating time. And specific methods are laid out for each step.

But, beyond its helpful methodology, *The Effective Executive* is a must-read because of Drucker's eloquent articulation of why effectiveness is so vital. Here's a sample:

> "The needs of large-scale organization have to be satisfied by common people achieving uncommon performance. This is what the effective executive has to make himself able to do. . . .
>
> "Developing executive effectiveness challenges directions, goals, and purposes of the organization. It raises the eyes of its people from preoccupation with problems to a vision of opportunity, from concern with weakness to exploitation of strengths."

Sadly, though it's been nearly three decades since the first publication of *The Effective Executive*, many of us have yet to assimilate the lessons contained therein. But recently the book underwent the latest of many paperback reprints, so there's always hope.

95 tips for mental effectiveness

1. Stay physically fit, and you'll find it easier to be mentally fit.

2. Increase your vocabulary.

3. Be a lifelong learner.

4. Attend professional development programs.

5. Turn your car into a "rolling university" by listening to motivational and educational tapes on your way to and from work.

6. Practice concentrating your full attention on the matter at hand.

7. Intensify your involvement in a major hobby to achieve excellence in a field other than your profession.

8. Make lists of ideas for personal growth. Review them regularly to check your progress.

9. Take behavioral assessment tests to determine your strengths and weaknesses.

10. Explore healthy responses to anger.

11. Realize that although you can't control others, you can control your reactions to them.

12. Join professional or trade associations and become an active member.

13. Contribute volunteer time to community or charitable organizations. Get to know the people you're working with and helping.

14. Mentor with successful role models.

15. Tune into cable channels you don't ordinarily watch.

16. Keep a daily journal.

17. Encourage — and participate in — team learning in the workplace.

18. Stay in touch with your spiritual side.

19. Take a correspondence course.

20. Teach a course through the local Y or a continuing education program.

21. Write an article for a trade publication.

22. Subscribe to new publications on a variety of subjects.

23. Visit the public library weekly and check out books recommended by friends and book critics.

24. Learn at least one new word daily.

25. Watch an educational or motivational program while exercising.

26. Take time to talk to — and listen to — your children.

27. Read cross-cultural books and magazines to learn about global perspectives and concerns.

28. Have a conversation with a stranger.

29. Ask your co-workers about their families and their hobbies.

30. Try watching television with your eyes closed.

31. Take a different route to work and observe things along the way.

32. Force yourself out of your "comfort zone" on a regular basis.

33. Keep a notepad or mini tape recorder with you to record your thoughts and ideas.

34. Learn another language.

35. Travel to places you've never been. Visit pubs and museums; learn about the present as well as the past.

36. Take a vacation and actually relax.

37. See a play, musical, ballet or concert. Visit an art, history or technology museum.

38. Work crossword puzzles.

39. Play Scrabble.

40. Consult a dictionary and thesaurus regularly.

41. Make a list of the positive attributes of someone you don't like.

42. Watch at least one television news discussion program weekly.

43. Continually challenge yourself to come up with new ideas and create new possibilities for yourself and others.

44. Learn to draw.

45. Associate with people who are mentally fit. Seek new friends with interests that are different and perhaps challenging to your own. Work on projects with them.

46. Watch "Jeopardy."

47. Develop and maintain your sense of humor.

48. Don't obsess about things beyond your control.

49. Sharpen your writing and thinking skills by trying your hand at poetry, essays or fiction.

50. Challenge your old beliefs daily.

51. Put your goals in writing, and review them often.

52. Like yourself, and enjoy your own company.

53. Listen to inspirational music.

54. Look for the good in things.

55. Subscribe to at least one newsweekly.

56. Read two daily newspapers that offer different viewpoints.

57. Frequent bookstores and browse through areas not normally in your field of interest.

58. Develop positive self-talk and positive self-expectancy. Be optimistic.

59. Foster strong family relationships.

60. Begin a regular correspondence with a friend.

61. Write a letter to the editor of a newspaper or magazine on an issue you feel strongly about.

62. Interact with people in different fields.

63. Visit hospitals to realize what good shape you're in.

64. Avoid excessive use of alcohol and junk food, which can dull your senses.

65. Associate with a stimulating peer group.

66. Develop a relationship with someone who has achieved a goal to which you aspire.

67. Make bookstores and fitness centers your new haunts for happy hour.

68. Consider the other side of the story.

69. Think and speak well of your health. Talk about health problems only with your doctor.

70. Scan your radio for an interesting talk show.

71. Become involved in youth activities through tutoring or coaching.

72. Read a biography or autobiography of someone you admire.

73. Take a sabbatical.

74. Regularly plan personal renewal time for yourself.

75. Attend a lecture.

76. Offer encouragement and praise to co-workers and family members.

77. Play chess.

78. Earn a degree in a new area.

79. Learn to play a musical instrument.

80. Watch foreign films.

81. Develop your listening skills. Use them daily.

82. Take a computer class.

83. Stay in touch with customers, even when you don't want to sell them anything. Find out all you can about them and build a database.

84. Develop a reading list, fiction as well as non-fiction.

85. Recognize stress, and find ways to reduce it in your life.

86. Try cross-training in different sports. Learn the rules to a new game.

87. Write a "legacy statement" describing what you hope to leave behind to your family, peers, community and profession.

88. Complete a puzzle of some kind.

89. Meditate. Use visualization to project yourself toward your goals.

90. Discipline yourself to tackle difficult tasks without procrastinating.

91. Work to improve your recall abilities, including remembering people's names.

92. Make a personal financial plan.

93. Constantly confront the things you fear. Ask yourself why you fear these things.

94. Use a daily planner or calendar.

95. Eliminate negativity from your life.

For further reading . . .

Ackoff, Russell L. *The Art of Problem Solving* (Wiley). This book provides a systematic approach to solving business problems, illustrated by "Ackoff's Fables," case studies of real-life business situations.

Adams, James L. *The Care and Feeding of Ideas: A Guide to Encouraging Creativity* (Addison Wesley). This book is "a guide to creating a greenhouse environment in which ideas can thrive" — in yourself and in your organization.

Albrecht, Karl. *Brain Power: Learn to Improve Your Thinking Skills* (Simon & Schuster). Albrecht provides a guide to improving six "functional skills" of thinking: "fact finding," "crap detecting," "thinking on your feet," "idea production," "problem solving and decision making" and "happying" — a new verb coined "to imply that one *does* happiness rather than *has* it."

Barker, Joel Arthur. *Future Edge: Discovering the New Paradigms of Success* (Morrow). This book is perhaps the most effective introduction to an important element of thinking more effectively: becoming aware of our own paradigms, the very ways in which we see the world

Covey, Stephen R. *The Seven Habits of Highly Effective People* (Simon & Schuster). Habit 2, "Begin with the End in Mind: Principles of Personal Leadership," offers good advice on realigning thinking patterns toward greater effectiveness.

de Bono, Edward. *Six Thinking Hats* (Little Brown). This accessible book, by the guru of "lateral thinking," presents six separate modes of thinking, each identified, for mnemonic purposes, with a different colored "hat."

Deep, Sam, and Lyle Sussman. *Yes, You Can!* (Seminars by Sam Deep). Chapter 1, "Think Positively," includes lists of tips on how to think more clearly and productively.

Denton, D. Keith, and Charles Boyd. *Did You Know? Fascinating Facts and Fallacies about Business* (Prentice Hall). Thinking effectively requires accurate information. This book demolishes hundreds of pieces of conventional wisdom, replacing them with the real story.

Fromm, Bill. *The Ten Commandments of Business and How to Break Them* (Berkley). This iconoclastic survey of contemporary business practices encourages new ways of thinking about generally accepted principles.

Harrison, Allen F., and Robert M. Bramson. *The Art of Thinking* (Berkley). This book outlines five different thinking styles, each appropriate for different occasions: the synthesist, the idealist, the pragmatist, the analyst and the realist.

Perkins, D.N. *The Mind's Best Work* (Harvard). This is an important textbook on creativity, loaded with "personal experiments" to engage the reader in new techniques for creative thinking.

Peters, Tom. *The Tom Peters Seminar: Crazy Times Call for Crazy Organizations* (Vintage). Chapter 2, "Beyond Decentralization: Disorganizing to Unleash Imagination," shows how transforming business structures can boost creative thinking.

Raudsep, Eugene. *How Creative Are You?* (Perigee). This book includes a test for measuring ten different creativity factors, and tips for removing personal blocks, problem-solving blocks and environmental blocks to creativity.

Rubin, Theodore Isaac. *Overcoming Indecisiveness: The Eight Stages of Effective Decision-Making* (Avon). This book by a leading psychotherapist provides a handy recipe for getting past "decision blockers" and becoming more decisive at home and at work.

Senge, Peter M. *The Fifth Discipline: The Art and Practice of the Learning Organization* (Doubleday). Senge provides a powerful introduction to new ways of thinking about organizations and their work.

von Oech, Roger. *A Whack on the Side of the Head: How You Can Be More Creative* (Warner). This book is a wonderful collection of fresh, specific techniques for coming up with new ideas. Also have a look at von Oech's *Whack Pack,* a deck of cards based on this book.

Waitley, Denis. *Timing is Everything: Turning Your Seasons of Success into Maximum Opportunities* (Nelson). Chapter 6, "The Season for Surveying the Challenge Ahead," provides clear guidelines for taking a personal inventory and surveying the landscape around you.

REFINE WORK HABITS

CHAPTER

S he dropped him like a bad habit."

This expression conveys the image of someone ending a relationship suddenly and decisively. The unwanted boyfriend may be quickly dispatched, but dropping a bad habit can be much more difficult and time-consuming. Anyone who has tried to quit smoking or modify the diet can attest to that.

What about our work habits? They can be changed for the better, but just like cigarette or dessert habits, those bad work habits can be difficult to break. In fact, "break" may not even be the right word to use. Denis Waitley likes to say that bad habits should not be broken — they should be replaced with good habits.

Don't worry about the time it takes. If you continue working toward replacing that bad habit, you'll get there — just as surely as I made those cross-country drives without having the destination in sight. In this chapter, I'll focus on refining work habits that can make a big difference in your productivity and satisfaction.

Take care of yourself. I consider staying in good physical condition an important work habit. The old saying is that if you have your health, you have just about everything. I don't quite agree with that. You may not have "everything" if you have your health, but if you *don't* have your health, nothing else will matter very much. See your doctor, and set up an exercise plan.

Each issue of *Lessons in Leadership*, a monthly subscription publication produced by WYNCOM, contains a department titled "A Day in the Life of . . .," which describes a typical day of a person who has demonstrated leadership qualities. (I've included some of these descriptions in this book.) Every person profiled has mentioned exercise as an important part of his or her day — and, believe me, these people are busy! But they mention an early-morning swim or a lunchtime run as being an important part of their lives.

> "Nothing in the world can take the place of persistence. Talent will not; nothing is more common than unsuccessful men with talent. Genius will not; unrewarded genius is almost a proverb. Education will not; the world is full of educated derelicts. Persistence and determination alone are omnipotent. The slogan 'press on' has solved and always will solve the problems of the human race."
> — Calvin Coolidge

Exercise is a wonderful stress-reducer. In fact, if you feel a lot of stress on your job and have not been exercising regularly, put the exercise program at the top of your list of priorities. Don't complain to the boss, request reassignment or think of changing jobs due to stress until you've tried regular exercise. If you have trouble finding the time for exercise, this chapter and Chapter 4 will be of help. Remember, see your doctor before beginning any exercise program.

Now let's go on to some other work habits that often need refining.

PERSISTENCE

Persistence is a great habit. We all had it as children, didn't we? If you're a parent now, you know just how persistent a child can be. In our work, we have to be persistent in a constructive, positive way. Some of us never developed our qualities of persistence beyond crying and holding our breath — and that just doesn't work very well in the business world.

"Nothing in the world can take the place of persistence," Calvin Coolidge said. And it's true that persistence can give you the opportunity to overcome long odds against success. Here are some more examples of persistence:

- Abraham Lincoln lost no fewer than eight elections for various offices before being elected president in 1860.

- Michael Jordan was cut from his junior high school basketball team.

- A businessman who once rented an office above a boat showroom and furnished it with one desk and two chairs is now chairman of a multi-million dollar company that works with today's leading authors and speakers on personal and professional development. (I confess, that businessman is me. Basketball was my first love, and this will probably be as close as Larry Holman's name ever gets to Michael Jordan's. But you get my point!)

- Turning the tables, the same businessman experienced persistence when Rose Frazier Cord, WYNCOM's Chief Operating Officer and Chief Financial Officer, and Earlene Dailey, our Special Projects Coordinator, refused to let him kill the idea of our November 1995 program featuring Stephen Covey, Tom Peters, Denis Waitley and moderator Linda Ellerbee. With all the other projects in the works, I thought we had enough business on our plates. But Rose and Earlene were absolutely dogged in their determination that this event take place. And then the rest of the organization got behind them to ensure that the event — the biggest in the company's history — would be a success.

I greatly value the intelligence of WYNCOM employees. As I've said many times in company meetings, "I'm just glad to be on the team." And I really feel that way. We have people who have expertise in a wide range of areas. But on the subject of persistence (or stubbornness, as some people who have tried to tell me "no" in the past might see it), I think I can claim something approaching expert status. Now that the company has reached its current status, it may be difficult to visualize the times that Arthur Light, my longtime associate, and I stuffed envelopes in my basement to market a local seminar. I knew I had a good idea; at times, I wasn't exactly sure what to do with it. But I knew giving up wouldn't help.

How do you develop persistence? The best way is to have worthy goals — goals that generate enthusiasm every time you think about them. To develop those goals, you must have a clear idea of your personal and professional priorities. It's difficult, maybe impossible, to stay focused on an idea you don't believe in. Determining priorities and setting goals that go along with those priorities will set the stage for persistence.

> "Long-range planning does not deal with future decisions, but with the future of present decisions."
> — Peter F. Drucker

Make time to think — *really* think — about those priorities. (See Chapter 4 again if you need help in finding the time to think.) Write down five personal priorities and five professional priorities. Do not be concerned with any obstacles at this point. The purpose of writing these ideas down is for you to determine your true priorities. For example, if continuing your formal education is really important to you, don't omit that from your list just because you're not sure how you will find the time or money to do it. You certainly don't need to have all the answers in place before you affirm your priorities. Don't be like the couple in their 90s who decided to get a divorce. When the judge asked them why they wanted to divorce at such an advanced age, their answer was, "We wanted to wait until the children died."

Remember, at this point, you're just trying to determine what's really important to you. We'll discuss goals and plans shortly. Priorities are the foundation on which your goals, your plans and your persistence must be built. As

> "Find the good in people and praise it."
> — Alex Haley

you go, you'll see where the larger ideas need to be broken down into smaller, more detailed plans. You don't have to show these priorities to anyone, and it may be better if you don't. It's always easy to find someone who will tell you that you can't possibly succeed. If you want to tell someone, make sure it is someone you deeply trust and respect.

Now you're ready to refine a second habit — *planning*. Persistence and planning go hand in hand.

PLANNING

Baseball Hall-of-Famer Yogi Berra has long been known for his unique way of expressing himself. He says things that sound funny at first, but usually are right on target. He summed up the problem of getting into a popular restaurant by saying, "Nobody goes there anymore. It's too crowded." He described playing left field in the afternoon shadows at Yankee Stadium by saying, "It gets late early out there." The statement might at first seem nonsensical, but after a second look, the point becomes clear.

Here's Yogi's thought on having a plan: "If you don't know where you're going, you might wind up someplace else." If you don't plan where you want to go with your life, you'll indeed wind up "someplace else." Entire books have been written on goal-setting. It's a topic that's worth further exploration, but for now let me get you started with a simple system.

Have daily and monthly to-do lists, and one-year and five-year plans for your career and your personal life. Make sure the daily and monthly lists always have an item or two related to the long-range plans. It's the same principle we talked about earlier: Stay on course and keep moving, and you will reach your destination.

"Ask yourself the question, 'What do I want to accomplish today?' Most people never ask it. People who fail never plan. Remember nothing becomes dynamic until it first becomes specific."
— Charles M. Simmons, *The Magic Key*,
quoted in *How to Make a Habit of Succeeding*,
by Mack R. Douglas

The monthly list will be less detailed than the daily list, and it will have more of a long-term flavor to it. The one-year and five-year plans should be reviewed at least monthly just to keep those ideas fresh in your mind — more often if you're losing your focus or changing your priorities. Be as specific as you can — don't say "I want a better job," "I want to make more money," or "I want to spend more time with my family." *Which* job do you want? What is *keeping* you from getting that job? *How much* more money do you need and want to make? *How many* more hours per week would you like to spend with your family? Stating your goals in a more specific form will allow you to fine-tune them as you move closer to accomplishing them. Having a worthy goal is critical to finding the motivation needed to consistently give your best effort.

On your lists, have a means of identifying the most important items. You could number them, although that sometimes results in several "number ones." One of my associates at WYNCOM uses a simple color-coded system in which the items to be done are written in blue ink, and the high-priority items are indicated with a red marker. He records the action taken on each item in black ink or pencil next to the original item. "Action taken" may not sound like planning, but it is. You're planning for those times when someone asks you what you did about a certain problem. You'll have the answer, if you file your to-do lists.

That leads into the next work habit to be refined: *preparation*.

PREPARATION

Filing your to-do lists makes it much easier to prepare for presentations, busy seasons or other recurring work. You can review what you did the last time that work was done. This way, you won't have to re-invent the wheel. It will free you to use your thinking time more creatively — making you even better prepared.

The Miami Dolphins' Don Shula, the all-time winningest coach in the National Football League, wants his players to be on "autopilot" during a game. In this case, "autopilot" means the players thoroughly know what they're supposed to do on every play the Dolphins call. They can run the plays without thinking.

"You can tell when a team is up for peak play, even before a game," Shula writes in *Everyone's a Coach*, which he co-authored with Ken Blanchard. "All their energy is going toward playing their best, working together. None of their attention is being drained away by worry about mechanical trifles — 'what-do-I-do-whens.' . . . When a person's on autopilot, the mental picture he carries matches the potential moves his body will make as the play comes off. He is not thinking of these things. He is simply doing what he has seen and felt a thousand times as he has run through this play in practice. . . . Then his mind can be thinking ahead, anticipating the opportunity to make something important happen."

> "It is wonderful how putting down on paper a clear statement of a case helps one to see, not perhaps the way out, but the way in."
> — A.C. Benson

Think about it. You're giving an important presentation when someone interrupts with a question. If you have prepared to the point that you're on "autopilot" for the basic presentation, you will be able to divert from your prepared remarks, answer the question, and perhaps even jump ahead in the presentation without missing a beat if you can see that your audience is ready for you to do so. As Don Shula might say, you are ready to make something important happen.

ORGANIZING YOUR MIND AND YOUR WORKSPACE

Devising worthwhile goals involves clear thinking, in terms both of analyzing and of taking advantage of your intuitive skills.

There are three tools that can enhance your thought potential and thus your effectiveness quotient -- by helping you create an "inner" environment that stimulates both the analytical and creative parts of your problem-solving, goal-setting processes. The three tools are:

1. Organizing your physical surroundings.

2. Organizing your mental surroundings.

3. Taking time to relax. (OK, I'll say it: To play!)

Organizing your physical surroundings. The best place to start is your desk. While the advantages of a pristine desktop are debatable (one leader's mess may be another leader's masterpiece), it's a safe bet that most clutter is an impediment. If you have a hard time finding things, if clutter is hampering your ability to organize your day or your planning, if important things are buried among the unimportant . . .

. . . with that kind of clutter, take no prisoners.

First, eliminate items that are not absolutely necessary (for example, are old memos and magazines you've been intending to read mixed in with more important paper work?). Next, vow never to let things get in such a state again. To keep the pledge, use the "single-handling" concept – i.e., whenever possible, don't handle a piece of paper more than once. If it requires action, take care of it immediately. If it doesn't, throw it away.

Next, check your files. Are they arranged to serve the purpose of files? Do they make it easier for you to find information when you need it? If not, establish a system that will do so. Also identify files that are obsolete and throw them away.

Organizing your mental surroundings. Often, physical clutter is merely a symptom of mental clutter, the stuff that keeps your creativity hidden behind a wall of confused or tentative thought. That often results in one of the most deadly foes of effectiveness: procrastination.

Establishing a list of goals and priorities before each workday will help you re-establish. I've already discussed the benefits of to-do lists, which can take many forms, such as the color-coded system that one of my associates uses. Another variation on the theme is the ABC system developed by Alan Lakein, author of *How to Get Control of Your Time and Your Life*. After listing the day's activities, assign them a priority:

"A" – "Should do now" – high payoff related to a critical goal and/or critical to successful performance. Critical and urgent.

"B"– "Should do soon" – high payoff and/or critical to successful performance, but can be temporarily postponed if necessary. Important, not urgent.

"C" – "Nice to do" – desirable but not critical to successful performance. Medium or low payoff. May be urgent, but not important.

Then, rank each item by priority: A-1, A-2, A-3..B-1, B-2 . . . etc. In an eight-hour workday, reserve no more than six work hours to "A" items. If these items require more time, review each one to see whether it really deserves an "A." If you don't finish with all the A's, congratulate yourself. You've still taken on the most important things and are well on your way. You'll find you get to the Bs as necessary, and that many of the Cs fall away all together. And if they eventually transform into As, you'll know it and deal with it then.

Taking time to relax. Stress and fatigue create their own form of clutter, which compromises your mental alertness. Not only is it easier to organize when rested and "light," it also sets the tone for creative thought to enter. Take time before and after work not just for planning, but also for time completely devoid of work considerations. It might involve quiet meditation, reading a few pages of a fun or interesting book or playing the card game on the computer.

Fun is not a four-letter word. Allow yourself some of it. Even allow it to interrupt your workday. Much like pulling off the interstate for a brief rest stop makes you more alert for the drive ahead, taking a mental pit stop during the workday can gear you up for the drive for effectiveness that lies ahead.

Organizing the mind and workspace – plus giving yourself time to relax and enjoy a moment away from the day's challenges – will help you refine your work habits, be prepared and stay prepared, creating the backdrop you need for effective self-leadership.

REFINING WORK HABITS THROUGH LIFELONG LEARNING

Another excellent way to be prepared and stay prepared is to be a lifelong learner. Denis Waitley likes to ask his seminar audiences, "In what year did you complete your education?" He says many people automatically write down the year of their high school or college graduation. The answer he looks for is: "I haven't completed my education. I'm still learning every day."

Use your new and improved time-management skills to continue learning. As Denis says, "The United States has the world's richest supply of free educational materials. Our libraries and university extension programs bulge with enough data to make anyone willing to spend the equivalent of a half-hour each evening both knowledgeable and successful. It's here and it's free – and yet it's still 'too hard' for many Americans to take advantage of this wonderful opportunity."

Even as you refine your work habits and begin to meet your goals, you'll need some positive reinforcement. Family and friends can help, but even those closest to you have their own lives to manage. You can provide your own motivation through affirmations. I have found affirmations to be an effective way to stay on the path toward accomplishment of my goals. Affirmations are statements that put your goals in the present tense, giving you an idea of the satisfaction you'll feel when you accomplish them. One I'm using often these days is "My best time for the marathon is three-and-a-half hours." Not "will be" or "should be," but "is." One I used until recently was "I am the author of a book on leadership." It's no longer a personal affirmation. It's a statement of fact, and it is just as satisfying as I thought it would be!

WORDS FROM WYNCOM

"By always realizing that each day is another opportunity to learn, and realizing I will never know a job so well there is nothing left to gain, I not only always complete each job fully, but follow up to ensure nothing was missed."
– *Anna Chapman*

"I try to learn by my mistakes and others as well. When I see someone who has an attitude that they know their job really well and they begin to think that their job is the most important, that is always a reminder to me that we all contribute an important piece of an outstanding puzzle, and if one falls, we all feel it. I try to come in with a smile, and do the best that I can and help others. I can control that; I cannot control others' behaviors or attitudes. And attitude is where it all starts, so have a good one!" – *Mary Kessler*

"Many times I will watch others to see how they get things done. When I find a more efficient way of doing things, I will try to implement it into my work habits. If it doesn't fit in with my personality or style, I will throw it out and look for new options. I also rely on tips from others and am open to others for suggestions. If I always think my way is best, my work habits will never change."
– *Kyle Bixler*

"Perform your most difficult task at a time when you have your fewest interruptions, so you can better concentrate on your task." –*Carl Swieterman*

"Prioritizing is the constant challenge I face with my responsibilities. I've learned to plan my days by setting necessary mini- and long-range goals. I've also learned how essential it is to be flexible." – *Anna Lee Ginter*

"I have tried to improve my work habits by starting my day earlier. I have found that I work better in the morning. I also have a schedule and set pattern to my work. I stick to this because, as I work in the schedule longer, I tend to become quicker at it."
– *Melissa Fightmaster*

"I try to improve my work habits by asking questions. I also watch what other people are doing. Sometimes just by watching how people do their jobs, you can learn a more effective way to do yours. Learning what other people do can be effective, too. You may learn that something you are doing is not needed for their part of the job." – *Gretchen Witham*

'Be quick, but don't hurry': an effective game plan

By Jim Harrick

"Be quick, but don't hurry." That was part of Coach John Wooden's philosophy as he led UCLA to ten national championships, and I kept it in mind as our 1995 UCLA team won the title. It may sound contradictory, but that phrase contains two distinct ideas that really fit together. "Be quick" refers to being alert, being able to execute and being able to react effectively to situations as they arise. "Don't hurry" means do all of those things in a controlled manner, taking full advantage of the preparation that went into the game plan.

A "game plan" is just that: a well-developed approach to a game – or a business matter. Coach Wooden and I strongly believe the time spent in practice is the key to success in the game. No matter what business you're in, the daily effort you make leading up to the important presentation, meeting or event will have a big effect. It will allow you to move "quickly," but without "hurrying."

To get the most out of practice time, Coach Wooden wrote out a detailed schedule, dividing the practice into 5-, 10-, or 15-minute segments for each drill. Do you have an equally good idea of how to spend your workday? It may not be necessary for you to divide the day into such short segments, but you should have definite ideas about what you want to accomplish each day. If you've never made a thorough study of time management, you should.

I want my players to set long-range, medium-range and short-range goals. Then I want to know *how they will accomplish those goals. That's the key.* If a player says his goal is to be a better shooter, will he actually make time and take time to come to the gym and shoot thousands of extra shots? Do you have a worthwhile goal, but no plan on how to reach it?

Before the season, I give each player a card on which I put his strengths, his weaknesses and my expectations. I tell him, "Here's what you need to do to improve." A lot of guys want to be All-American but don't want to work like All-Americans.

Of course, the coach needs to improve, too! When I give the players their cards, I also give them an opportunity to ask any question they want. I want to know: What do I have to do to make you a better player? How can I coach you better? What motivates you? What do I do that you like — and dislike?

With planning and practice, you can move toward maximum effectiveness. And you can do it quickly, without hurrying.

For further reading . . .

Clemens, John K., and Steve Albrecht. *The Timeless Leader* (Adams). Chapter 1, "Leaving the Comfort Zone," draws on Plato's "allegory of the cave," as well as several modern corporations, for lessons on change.

Covey, Stephen R. *Principle-Centered Leadership* (Summit). Chapter 5, "A Break with the Past," discusses the three forces — appetites and passions, pride and pretension, aspiration and ambition — that block change, and makes five powerful suggestions for changing bad habits.

Covey, Stephen R. *The Seven Habits of Highly Effective People* (Simon & Schuster). Part 1, "Paradigms and Principles," is an excellent overview of changing habits from "inside-out" by changing paradigms.

de Bono, Edward. *Six Action Shoes* (Harper). This sequel to *Six Thinking Hats* proposes six styles of action, each illustrated by a shoe type: navy formal shoes, grey sneakers, brown brogues, orange gumboots, pink slippers and purple riding boots.

Deep, Sam, and Lyle Sussman. *Yes, You Can!* (Seminars by Sam Deep). While this entire book can be read as a guide to refining work habits, Chapter 2, "Act Powerfully," is an especially helpful inventory of techniques for doing so.

Hammer, Michael, and Steven A. Stanton. *The Reengineering Revolution: A Handbook* (Harper Business). This important guide to restructuring business processes contains many insights that are applicable to individual, as well as organizational, "reengineering."

Jordan, Michael. *I Can't Accept Not Trying: Michael Jordan on the Pursuit of Excellence* (Harper). This handsome little book provides short, powerful statements on goals, fears, commitment, teamwork, fundamentals and leadership.

Milteer, Lee. *Feel and Grow Rich: How To Inspire Yourself To Get* Anything *You Want* (Hampton Roads). This book challenges the reader to "take back your life," and includes a 21-day "success fitness plan."

Noe, John R. *Peak Performance Principles for High Achievers* (Berkley). This book outlines the six essential attitudes of high achievers: They "make no small plans," "are willing to do what they fear," "are willing to prepare," "are willing to risk failure," "are teachable" and "have heart."

Peters, Tom. *The Pursuit of WOW! Every Person's Guide to Topsy-Turvy Times* (Vintage). While the entire book is about changing work habits, the chapter titled "Pens, Toilets, and Businesses That Do It Differently" is an especially good place to find examples of radically divergent approaches to business.

Peters, Tom. *The Tom Peters Seminar: Crazy Times Call for Crazy Organizations* (Vintage). Chapter 1, "Beyond Change: Toward the Abandonment of Everything," and Chapter 9, "Beyond Change (Redux): Toward Perpetual Revolution," frame this book about revolutionizing the way our culture does business.

Sheehy, Gail. *Passages: Predictable Crises of Adult Life* (Bantam). Changing habits is easier if we understand the other changes that we all go through as we grow. This book documents the stages in the adult life cycle.

Waitley, Denis. *Being the Best: A Life-Changing Guide to* Real *Success* (Pocket Books). Chapter 9, "Passion, Practice, and Perseverance," is an excellent short introduction to changing habits by replacing them.

Waitley, Denis. *Empires of the Mind: Lessons to Lead and Succeed in a Knowledge-Based World* (Morrow). Chapter 11, "Self-Leadership and Skills: Your Winning (and Losing) Habits," offers encouragement and advice for changing long-established behaviors.

Waitley, Denis. *Timing is Everything: Turning Your Seasons of Success into Maximum Opportunities* (Nelson). Chapter 11, "The Season for Effort," provides help on consistency and quality of performance, and Chapter 13, "The Season for Endurance," is a good discussion of perseverance.

KEEP UP WITH INFORMATION

CHAPTER

In 1995, Denis Waitley, the author/narrator of the all-time best-selling personal development audio program in the world, dedicated his latest book, *Empires of the Mind: Lessons to Lead and Succeed in a Knowledge-Based World*, to WYNCOM.

Besides acknowledging the long-standing professional relationship with WYNCOM as a distinguished speaker for our Lessons In Leadership series, Denis made this dedication because he felt that the company exemplifies one of the major themes in his book: Highly successful organizations of the future will be based upon information. WYNCOM is a company created and driven by the mind: It manufactures no hard goods, harvests no crops and mines no coal from the hills of Kentucky where it is located. Each WYNCOM employee, as Denis points out in his dedication, embodies the new potential of the coming information revolution.

According to Alvin and Heidi Toffler, in their book *Creating a New Civilization*, this new revolution is now upon us. The Tofflers argue that history is not the stuff of class struggle, but technological innovation, occurring in waves. The agricultural revolution, which resulted in feudal-style social systems, was the First Wave. The Second was the Industrial Revolution, which led to vast societal upheaval and change. Now breaking upon us is the Third Wave, a time when the basis for wealth and power will be information. Information will, according to these authors, force a complete overhaul of everything, from family life to political systems.

Peter Drucker, one of the preeminent business and management writers of our time, gives three reasons that organizations will have to become information-based. First is demographic — the knowledge workers who increasingly make up the work force will no longer adhere to the methods of the past. Second is the need to systematize innovation, which is now essentially knowledge work. Finally is the requirement to come to terms with information technology. A company, Drucker argues, must decide what relevance and purpose information has for it.

> "Americans today are no better prepared for the new ways of earning a living in the emerging economy they face than 18th-century English yeomen were at the dawn of the Industrial Age."
> — William Bridges, author of *Job Shift*

DEFINING INFORMATION

Information is the creative energy of the universe, states Margaret Wheatley in her book *Leadership and the New Science*. Wheatley argues that we've treated information as a "thing, as an inert entity to disseminate," and that this has gotten us into trouble. Subscribing to this theory only demonstrates that we don't understand information.

Information, Wheatley suggests, is not a concrete, stable entity. "It is not the limited, quantifiable, put-it-in-a-memo-and-send-it-out commodity with which we have become so frustrated. In new theories of evolution and order, information is a dynamic element, taking center stage. It is information that gives order, that prompts growth, that defines what is alive. It is both the underlying structure and the dynamic process that ensure life."

"In a constantly evolving, dynamic universe," she continues, "information is the fundamental ingredient, the key source of structuration — the process of creating structure. Something we cannot see, touch, or get our hands around is out there, organizing life. Information is managing us."

APPROACHING ANXIETY

Despite the elegance of Wheatley's definition, the changing dynamic of information does not sit easy with most of us. Aware of this fact, author and entrepreneur Richard Saul Wurman coined the phrase "information anxiety," defining it as "the ever-widening gap between what we understand and what we think we should understand. Information anxiety is the black hole between data and knowledge."

Earlene Dailey, project coordinator for WYNCOM's 1995 teleconference team, put it more simply: "I read all the time, study all the time. But at times there is so much information coming in, there's no way to keep up. It can be overwhelming."

Information anxiety is often associated with the ever-invasive computer, the most pervasive symbol of the Information Age. Authors such as Nicholas Negroponte in *Being Digital* point out that an escalating line of ever-smarter computers are on the way to our businesses and even our homes. Despite the facility that most of us in the workplace have gained with computers and technology over the past decade, we are often made to feel like idiots in our attempts to make better use of that technology. Looking through the shelves in the local bookstore can convince you that while you must keep up with information, you must also have the intellectual competence of a number-two lead pencil for trying to do so. Take a look at such titles as *DOS for Dummies, The Complete Idiot's Guide to Multimedia* and *The Internet for Dummies.* But our belief, that as the computers get smarter, we will have less to do in keeping up with information, simply isn't true.

INFORMATION INTERVENTION

Everyone faces the challenge of keeping up with information. For WYNCOM's Chief Operating Officer and Chief Financial Officer, Rose Frazier Cord, it's making necessary projections to create a five-year plan for the company. For Veronica Embs in registration, it's learning a new software package.

Everyone is looking for perspective. What do I need? How do I sort through so much material? How do I keep up with the changes? What is really important?

Add to these questions the fact that most information does not come purely as information. Instead, it is often wrapped in opinion and perceptions. These create a needed diversity of thought, but may also be problematic in maintaining a clear focus. A water lily blooming on a lake may present a scene of beauty, but if allowed to overtake the surface, the plants will deplete the entire lake.

> "I go over the numbers every day from 4 to 6 p.m. I know entrepreneurs who say they'll look at the numbers at the end of the year. Never wait till the end of the year, or you'll learn about trouble too late to act."
>
> — Courtland "Corky" L. Logue, Austin, Texas, quoted in *Fortune* magazine July 10, 1995

Many have discovered that having more information does not necessarily resolve problems more easily, bring results more quickly or lead to more creative avenues of thinking.

Perhaps the first step in resolving the dilemma of keeping up with information is coming up with a different attitude toward it. If we are to survive and thrive in the Information Age, we need to admit that information has changed, our relationship to it has changed, and our addiction to controlling it may be more of a liability than an asset. If we can adopt an attitude of staying open to the changing nature of information, becoming agents of that change, we can then learn to creatively adjust to the uncertainty and ambiguity inherent in this new era.

Adopting such an attitude can make the challenge of information access easier. Today, with so much information available, complexity comes easily, often accompanied by confusion. It can be argued that this fact is a result of our insistence on linear thinking, rather than considering other approaches that may actually be more effective. Some of these other approaches to information are more associative, relationship-based and free-form than systematic in nature. Edward de Bono, in *Serious Creativity*, describes this as *lateral thinking*, "the searching for different approaches and different ways of looking at things."

Scientists postulate that these different types of thinking come from different parts of the brain, and may be used differently by the different sexes. Women, according to John Gray in *Men Are From Mars, Women Are From Venus*, use relationship more in their communication style than men. There is no doubt, however, that only the tiniest part of the mind's abilities have been tapped.

CREATING COMMUNICATION FLOW

Keeping up with information on an organizational level can benefit from a similar shift in attitude. WYNCOM, as an organization, has attempted to create more open, flowing lines of communication than the traditional hierarchical company. Positions and roles are created around needs and goals. There are few given titles, except those created to meet legal and other external needs.

My wife, WYNCOM President Bunny Holman, puts it this way: "The neatest thing about our whole company is that anybody can be anything. When we first started out, we let everybody decide what they wanted to be called. I've never been anywhere that they let people do that. Most people go into a job where they don't have a whole lot of choice.

"The company is very flexible and open for people to move around as they grow, as they see opportunity or as they feel a need. We've had many situations where people create a position for themselves because they see a need for that position. Maybe it just didn't occur to us, because we're not doing those jobs every day. The philosophy of the company is that anybody can be whatever they want to be. And I think that makes us kind of special."

Just as this approach is creating a sense of excitement and newness at WYNCOM, it has also presented new opportunities for the flow of information at all levels. Because WYNCOM has grown rapidly from an organization small enough that everyone in the company could meet in a small room several times a day, to one that now relies on e-mail and other information systems for communication, there have also been challenges and transitions.

WYNCOM CEO Jerry Miller describes the process that the company has undergone. "The history of this company is that it was not unusual for the entire company to congregate in an office two or three times a day for a meeting that was basically 'here's where we are; here's what we have to do.' So every-

"All men, by nature, desire to know."
— Aristotle

one was absolutely connected to the latest information, into the latest challenge, and they all became a part of it directly.

"As companies get larger and find other ways to communicate, some of those ways begin to disconnect the people who are most important to the success of the business. The challenge that we have is to figure out a way, as we continue to grow, to prevent that disconnection from occurring."

One of the ways I've streamlined information flow in my own life is by going "paperless," not carrying even a calendar or to-do list. I realize, of course, that I have the luxury of having an excellent support staff, and that I have the great privilege of being married to a wondrously organized business partner. And I realize that for many people, a calendar and to-do lists are important tools for simplifying, rather than complicating, their lives. But I thrive on the freedom I get from not being a slave to paper.

My friend Ken Davis, a regular WYNCOM consultant, while never without his calendar and to-do list, has found other ways to diminish his paper overload. He finds, for example, that he can do totally without daily newspapers, getting the daily news he needs from National Public Radio, the more detailed analysis of that news from weekly publications (most often *The Economist*), and what he calls the "real news" from a wide variety of monthly and quarterly magazines, some popular, some obscure.

BUILDING A LEARNING ORGANIZATION

One of the ways we've tried to use information at WYNCOM is by turning our company into a true "learning organization," one that feeds on information flow in order to continually improve and evolve. For us, that means, first of all, that we take full advantage of the incredible resource offered by the speakers whose programs we arrange: Stephen Covey, Michael Hammer, Tom Peters, Lyle Sussman and Sam Deep, Denis Waitley, Ken Blanchard and others.

Some of these speakers have developed new programs right in our WYNCOM offices, sitting down with a wide diversity of WYNCOM employees and throwing out ideas. While the primary purpose of these planning sessions is, of course, program development, their secondary impact is "employee development" within WYNCOM, exposing our people to the latest, sometimes unpolished, thinking of some of business's best minds.

That exposure continues and broadens at "dress rehearsals." Like some restaurants that preview their menus for employees, their relatives, and their friends on the night or nights before their grand openings, WYNCOM often previews its new programs for in-house audiences (sometimes expanded to include other important stakeholders such as our bankers). And even if we have to leave a skeleton crew behind to "watch the store," we make sure that those people get to one of the first public programs.

As a result of this shared exposure to the best current business thinking, WYNCOM employees have developed a shared conceptual base and a shared vocabulary. "Empowerment," for example, isn't just a faddish buzzword in our company; it's frequently heard because it has been internalized and *lived*.

But even beyond our own speakers, I'm always on the lookout for ways to keep informing and educating our organization. Early in WYNCOM's history, for example, I read, and was heavily influenced by, Tom Chappell's book, *The Soul of a Business*. Over the past few years, I've bought literally dozens of copies, to give to WYNCOM employees as they were hired. Tom's language of "circles" and "triangles" has become a part of the WYNCOM vocabulary. Similarly, I encourage WYNCOM employees to copy and circulate current articles that they find especially interesting or challenging. In our experience, these circulated articles and books don't add to "information overload." When they come accompanied by the personal care and endorsement of a friend, they can provide a refreshing break in the work day.

Sometimes learning opportunities have to be seized, literally "on the fly." A couple of years ago, I was delighted to find myself seated next to journalist Linda Ellerbee on a plane. Not far into our conversation, I realized that I was not the only WYNCOM employee who should be listening to what she was saying. By the end of the flight, we had managed to rearrange her schedule for the next day and reroute her into Lexington, where she spoke to the entire WYNCOM community.

When Humpty Dumpty talks with Alice about the use of words, he reminds her that "the question is . . . which is to be master — that's all." In my experience, that's the question that 20th and 21st century leaders and their organizations have to face in dealing with information. Do we let information master us, drowning us in its overload? Or do we master it, turning it to our use as learners, and as learning organizations?

WORDS FROM WYNCOM

"I just read everything I can get my hands on. I take three or four computer magazines, for example. It's not really 'work' to me, because I enjoy it. Pick something you enjoy and try to learn everything you can about it. When you see people doing things that you don't know how to do but that interest you, ask them to teach you. And read all you can: books, magazines, newspapers. I draw the line at the sports page. That's my husband's job: explaining all the sports I need to know about." – *Elaine Rutherford*

"In my area, public relations, there is so much information to stay abreast of, and things happen so quickly, it is a real challenge to keep myself informed. In order to stay focused and keep 'information overload' at bay, I process and prioritize data, skipping over the least important so that I have the ability to capture the most important facts. I scan articles, headlines and publications as quickly as possible. And only if they are pertinent or hold my interest do I read for details." – *Susan Miller*

For further reading . . .

Buckholtz, Thomas J. *Information Proficiency: Your Key to the Information Age* (Van Nostrand Reinhold). This helpful book suggests ways to make better use of the growing amount of information available, by "energizing the information resources community."

Campbell, Susan M. *From Chaos to Confidence: Survival Strategies for the New Workplace* (Simon & Schuster). This book argues that the key to business success is moving from "security/control" to "learning/discovery," and it suggests six "meta-skills" for doing so: "participate with the change process," "let go and go on," "focus on essentials," "communicate to build trust," "cultivate both/and thinking" and "be a team learner."

Case, John. *Open-Book Management: The Coming Business Revolution* (Harper Business). This revolutionary book proposes that opening financial information to all employees results in "the power of information," "the power of business literacy," "empowerment with brains" and "a stake in success."

Davidow, William H., and Michael S. Malone. *The Virtual Corporation* (Harper Business). Chapter 3, "Powers of Information," demonstrates the importance of information in present-day organizations.

McCarthy, Michael J. *Mastering the Information Age* (Jeremy Tarcher). This guide is perhaps the most complete available collection of practical strategies and tactics for coping with, and capitalizing on, information resources.

Peters, Tom. *The Pursuit of WOW! Every Person's Guide to Topsy-Turvy Times* (Vintage). Although much of this book deals with uses of information, Section 43 in particular is a good, brief challenge to eliminate information overload.

Peters, Tom. *The Tom Peters Seminar: Crazy Times Call for Crazy Organizations* (Vintage). The section "Let Your Imagination Soar," beginning on page 146, paints a fascinating picture of "networked brainfood on demand" as "an essential element of our national economic infrastructure."

Shula, Don, and Ken Blanchard. *Everyone's a Coach: You Can Inspire Anyone to Be a Winner* (Harper Business and Zondervan). Chapter 2, "Overlearning," deals with the uses of good information in sports and business.

Waitley, Denis. *Empires of the Mind: Lessons to Lead and Succeed in a Knowledge-Based World* (Morrow). Chapter 10, "Self-Leadership and Knowledge: Your Informed Touch," is a good discussion of balancing information power with personal power. "You must think like a high-tech research firm," Waitley says, "but act like a high-touch service firm."

Wheatley, Margaret J. *Leadership and the New Science: Learn-ing about Organization from an Orderly Universe* (Berrett-Koehler). Chapter 6, "The Creative Energy of the Universe — Information" points out how information, in a very real sense, creates reality — in the universe and in organizations.

Wurman, Richard Saul. *Information Anxiety: What to Do When Information Doesn't Tell You What You Need to Know* (Bantam). This entertaining book, by a talented entrepreneur and designer, gives fascinating approaches to preventing information overload, both as a sender and as a receiver of information.

BALANCE WORK & PERSONAL LIFE

Ask many of us to list the crucial problems of contemporary life and you can almost hear a collective sigh when one of the most important themes emerges: lack of balance. Many of us feel we are working too hard, worrying too much and exhausting ourselves in the process. Nearly everyone puts a priority on the intangibles of love, friendship and family, but in order to succeed in the business world, we may feel forced to shortchange loved ones and sacrifice personal life. It seems to happen overnight — just when our jobs and careers seem up and running toward success, our personal lives begin to ache from neglect.

As a runner, I know that each person has a target zone to maximize his or her conditioning. Sports medicine experts explain that when the target zone is continually reached, maintained and expanded, the body then adapts and makes changes. A combination of short bursts of running interspersed by walking seems more effective in triggering the target zone than a constant steady pace for the same period of time. Such target zones exist not only for the heart, but also for the brain. Balancing our work and personal lives can also be seen as a continual process of hitting the target zone and making adjustments, one that requires both desire and commitment.

Such a process may seem as difficult as an out-of-shape runner trying to compete in the Boston Marathon. (That's something I'm personally trying to overcome as I prepare for my first try at the famous run.) It often feels like a race that we are being forced into, one for which we have little desire or ambition. We begin to feel that the life we are living is not the one we chose. Or that the race is on a treadmill that never ends. Or that it's an amusement park horror: a roller coaster of highs and lows that leaves us confused and exhausted.

> "We are asking ourselves what is real, what is honest, what is quality, what is valued, what is really important. We are trading in the rewards of traditional success in favor of slower pace and quality of life."
> — Faith Popcorn, *The Popcorn Report*

Each of us may be able to identify with one or more of these patterns at different times in our careers. Elaine Rutherford, WYNCOM's customer relations coordinator — as well as a wife and the mother of a 4-year-old son and a 7-year-old daughter — is candid in describing the stress she sometimes feels in this balancing process:

"Sometimes you feel that you simply delegate your life to everyone else. You know it won't always be like that. There's a sense of pressure — often from your own mind as much as from others. I'm not a superwoman like you read about in the magazines. Sometimes people think you should get to work early, stay late, fix a three-course meal every night, clean the house and still want to do more.

"I'm fortunate to have a job that I really enjoy, that satisfies my need for personal expression. Sometimes everything is not great, but it works. You just have to continually decide what is right for you."

Deciding what is "right" for each of us may indeed be the fulcrum that supports the see-saw of work and personal balance. The problem for many of us is that it is too easy to get trapped in playing out the security, power and other myths that we have allowed to be programmed into the biocomputers that are our lives. We've accepted such myths as the no-fail career path, the company that will care for you and, as Elaine says, the popular notion that you can have it all and do it all.

This creates an imbalance in which we no longer "listen" to ourselves in regard to things that count. Instead, we simply buy into the myths, promises and realities that may work for others, but are not our own. We get hung up in the repetition of patterns that are based on someone else's sense of balance and success.

It's like the example of the rat in the maze. Put a rat in a maze with a series of tunnels. When you turn him loose at the entrances, he will sniff around, look them over, then perhaps randomly begin to explore each one until he finds the cheese. The next time you put the rat into the maze, there may be a certain amount of random behavior, but very quickly he goes down the tunnel with the cheese. After a few times, the rat will always directly go down the tunnel where he knows he will find the cheese. Take the cheese out, put the rat back at the entrance, and he will again go down the tunnel where he found the cheese before. He may even try this several times. But after a few trials, he will stop going down this tunnel, and start exploring other ones.

The difference between a rat and a human is that the rat will stop going down the tunnel where he doesn't get the reward he desires. A human, however, may continue down the same tunnel for his lifetime, looking for something that he knows is not there. Odd, when you think that a rat cannot go to the library and read about the latest trends to retrieve cheese, attend motivational presentations on how to have the right state of mind to get cheese, or even work with a team of fellow rats to brainstorm cheesy alternatives.

CAUSES OF IMBALANCE

When we find ourselves feeling trapped, a single question often arises: "What happened?" Trying to make sense of our lopsided predicaments, we demand more answers: "Aren't we giving everything we've got, working long hours, following all the perceived rules? Why aren't we getting what we hoped for? What has caused such imbalance in our lives?" Here are some possibilities:

1. Change

    a. Information anxiety

    b. Disruption in family life

   c. New social patterns

   d. Rapid shifts in world events

   e. Technological advances

2. Conflict

   a. Business restructuring

   b. Indecision about personal goals

   c. Community controversy

   d. Family discord

3. Materialism

   a. Supporting a lifestyle

   b. Keeping up with the Joneses

   c. Unrealistic expectations

   d. Needs rising to meet income

   e. Belief that value and security lie in possessions

4. Fear and worry (for help in this area, see Chapter 6!)

   a. Feeling no control over life

   b. Concern for the unknown

   c. Lack of self-esteem and confidence

   d. Inability to set priorities

   To take the first steps in resolving the causes of imbalance, answer, if you will, two basic questions: (1) Who am I? and (2) What is really important to me?

Starting here, you can enforce strategies to restore and maintain a sense of balance between business and personal life, becoming more fulfilled and productive in both environments.

The answer to "Who am I?" may be the most powerful influence on your behavior and the ability to balance your life. Psychologist Marsha Sinetar, in her book *Healing Choices, Elegant Choices,* states that to say who we are "means we must progressively develop a crisp sense of our own potentials and boundaries, that we pinpoint our cher-

> **"If you are like most people, you don't want a different life; you just want to feel successful in the one you've chosen."**
> — Steven Carter and Julia Sokol,
> *Lives Without Balance*

ished values as well as those rules, customs and beliefs that mean nothing to us." In answering this core question, we determine our individual definition of success and then decide how we want spend our time and energy in conducting our lives.

Carolyn Coffey, computer operations coordinator at WYNCOM, beautifully sums up this process: "I balance my work and personal life in several ways. I choose work that is honorable, and I never chase money for a career. I view work as a means of enhancing my personal life. I try to practice self-honesty. I recognize that unhappiness and discontent are usually the result of something I am not doing (and something which I probably would rather not face). I try to accept responsibility for my own happiness by supporting the positive actions in my life and being willing to try something different when my actions are negative."

While balanced self-leadership starts from within, organizations can also have a profound impact on people's ability to enjoy well-rounded lives while contributing their time and talents to the workplace. One outstanding example is the Longaberger Company of Dresden, Ohio, profiled in Tom Peters' monthly newsletter, *On Achieving Excellence.* Founded by Dave Longaberger in 1973 to sell his father's hand-woven hardwood baskets, the company has evolved into a direct-sales empire with 5,000 employees and 26,000 independent sales consultants. They are proof positive that the company's mission statement — To Stimulate a Better Quality of Life — is carried through on a daily basis.

Within its corporate environment, the Longaberger Company stresses the importance of communication with employees, job rotation to prevent burnout, and participatory management. Perhaps even more impressive is the company's sensitivity to employees' personal concerns. Benefits include an on-site clinic, free counseling through the Employee Assistance Program

> "It is pointless to attack life in a desperate frenzy. You'll never get out alive! Relax your way through. Try to make the world just a little bit better because you were there. Your time will be well spent if you do."
> — Merrill E. Douglass and Donna N. Douglass, *Manage Your Time, Your Work, Yourself*

and a day-care center providing inexpensive, reliable child care 22 hours a day.

Organizations of all sizes can take steps to help employees achieve balance in their lives. WYNCOM, as a young and rapidly growing company, recently implemented WYNCARE, a confidential off-site counseling service to which employees have access at no personal expense. Flex-time, job-sharing, child care subsidies, realistic maternity/paternity leaves — these are just some of the options that can be implemented to forge an employee/employer relationship of mutual trust and respect. By providing such services, companies can lower absenteeism, raise morale and motivate workers at all levels to devote their energies toward a common goal.

All individuals and organizations strive for success. While there are many variations on the concept of success, its achievement is a continuing process. The needs for self-awareness, developing focus and setting flexible priorities are all simply components of this larger process. When we keep this in mind, we can learn to adapt and change, finding the "target zone" of balance in our lives.

Words from WYNCOM

"I balance my work and personal life by setting priorities, knowing my limits, respecting personal boundaries, merging work and personal life when necessary and practicable." – *Anna Jarvis*

"You have to cut out everything but the most essential parts. Since my children are very young, it is necessary to put their wants and needs ahead of mine, but I know that when they are older, I will be able to spend more time pursuing my own interests. My job is so interesting that it satisfies my need for personal expression."
– *Elaine Rutherford*

"I try to accept responsibility for my own happiness by supporting the positive actions in my life and being willing to try something different when my actions are negative. When I need to concentrate on my personal goals, I take steps to ensure that I cannot hide in work, often by reaching out to friends and family. When I need to concentrate on work goals, I take steps to ensure that I have a greater sense of accomplishment, often by prioritizing." – *Carolyn Coffey*

"I think that the struggle to properly balance our work and personal life is lifelong. I think that stresses in both areas constantly call for adjustments. Often a major event either part time or negative causes us to reconsider and adjust our life. Balance is a constant goal for me."
– *Rita Cambron*

"Flexible hours help a lot; I am a morning person and usually work 7 a.m. to 3 p.m. and don't take lunch."
– *Susan Thacker*

"I try to give my family insight into my work. I try to give my work insight into my family. I feel the more interconnected these two aspects of my life are, the better they can coexist with each other. I try to be pleasing to both." – *Dan Lesher*

"I believe in Dr. Covey's advice to 'sharpen the saw.' Our spirit, mind, and body are what we contact this world with and it is important that all of these areas are constantly nourished and refreshed. If we take good care of these areas, we will be able to meet our other obligations and have a happy and harmonious life." – *Linda Rogers*

"You can balance your life by keeping the big picture in your mind at all times." –*Bob Benson*

For further reading . . .

Arterburn, Stephen. *Winning at Work Without Losing at Love* (Nelson). This book is a guide to balancing "the mission, the money, and the meaning of your life," with a major section devoted to each.

Bedrosian, Maggie. *Life Is More Than Your To-Do List: Blending Business Success with Personal Satisfaction* (BCI Press). This book offers a 28-day plan for balancing home and work lives.

Carter, Steven, and Julia Sokol. *Lives Without Balance: When You're Giving Everything You've Got and Still Not Getting What You Hoped For* (Villard). Filled with case studies and self-awareness questionnaires, this book is an excellent guide to "reclaiming your identity and writing your own definition of success."

Chappell, Tom. *The Soul of a Business: Managing for Profit and the Common Good* (Bantam). Chapter 9, "Managing — and Competing — by the Middle Way," describes the "middle way," a balance of profit and principle, pursued by Tom's of Maine.

Covey, Stephen R. *Principle-Centered Leadership* (Summit). Chapter 7, "The Seven Deadly Sins," outlines such out-of-balance situations as "pleasure without conscience," "knowledge without character" and "commerce without morality."

Covey, Stephen R. *The Seven Habits of Highly Effective People* (Simon & Schuster). Part Four, "Renewal," includes a thoughtful discussion of achieving balance in our lives.

Deep, Sam, and Lyle Sussman. *Yes, You Can!* (Seminars by Sam Deep). Chapter 7, "Prosper at Home," includes a number of helpful tips for balancing home and workplace.

Moore, Thomas. *Care of the Soul: A Guide for Cultivating Depth and Sacredness in Everyday Life* (Harper Collins). Much of this book's insight into cultivating the inner self has significant implications for finding balance between home and work.

Robertson, Arthur K., and William Proctor. *Work a Four-Hour Day: Achieving Business Efficiency on Your Own Terms* (Morrow). This book suggests defining priorities, understanding personal rhythms of effectiveness, and literally moving into "a four-hour workday that is satisfying to both you *and* your boss."

Sinetar, Marsha. *Elegant Choices, Healing Choices: Finding Grace and Wholeness in Everything We Choose* (Paulist Press). This book suggests ways of integrating one's whole self, in all life's activities.

Waitley, Denis. *Empires of the Mind: Lessons to Lead and Succeed in a Knowledge-Based World* (Morrow). Chapter 13, "Self-leadership and Love: Your Greatest Gift," applies self-leadership principles to intimate, family relationships.

USE THE POWER OF THE SELF- FULFILLING PROPHECY

CHAPTER

I knew it."

Depending on the voice inflection, that phrase can be the signal of success — or the announcement of failure. *Either way, it's a confirmation of what was expected.*

Picture the person speaking the words "I knew it." If the person is smiling, with hands upraised, then it can be assumed that he or she has confirmed a positive expectation. "I knew I was right about that." "I knew we could do it." If I were quoting that person in writing, I would put an exclamation point at the end of the sentence. "I knew it!"

Now picture someone saying "I knew it" with a downcast expression. "I knew I would fail." "I knew this wouldn't work." No exclamation point here. Still, expectations are confirmed, just as they were in the first example. Fortunately, we have the ability to control expectations.

Napoleon Hill wrote, "You have absolute control over but one thing — your thoughts. This divine prerogative is the sole means by which you may control your destiny. If you fail to control your mind, you will control nothing else. Your mind is your spiritual estate.

What you hold in your mind today will shape your experiences of tomorrow."

Your expectations — your "prophecies" about yourself — will have a powerful effect on your future. Let me emphasize that there are other factors. Hard work, preparation, continuing education, time management and other topics we've covered in this book will be important

---

"The way of the masters was to find their own way."
— Zen proverb

---

to your success. But think of the last major project you completed. Whether you categorize it as a rousing success, a total failure or somewhere in between, couldn't you have said "I knew it" upon completion of the work?

A POSITIVE PROCESS

Moving toward positive expectations and beliefs about ourselves and our work — and, by extension, about our teammates and their work — is a process. It's not an item on today's to-do list that can be accomplished and checked off. The first step toward raising your expectations is the same first step needed to form many of the habits of success: Determine what you want to do.

The late Earl Nightingale said: "It's been said that Americans can have anything they want; the trouble is that they don't know what they want."

If you honestly don't know what you want, review the goal-setting process in Chapter 8. Remember to narrow down concepts like "a lot of money," "a big house," "more time for hobbies." As you cut those broad ideas down to manageable size, your goal will come into focus — and you're on your way. If money seems to be the biggest obstacle, think again about the idea presented in Chapter 2: If you help others meet their goals, you will be very valuable to them. Of course, as important as that first step is, there is a long way between knowing what you want to do with your life and actually doing it.

Maybe you're at this stage: You meet an old friend, perhaps a high school classmate at a reunion. He asks what you're doing now, and you tell him about your job. He asks, "Do you like it?"

At this point, the self-discipline of a double agent couldn't keep you from feeling that little knot inside. It's the knowledge that you've let go of your dreams without giving your best effort and settled for something less. But you overcome that little knot

> "The greatest tragedy in life is people who have sight but no vision."
> — Helen Keller

and give him an acceptable answer. After all, you've had plenty of practice. Then your friend unwittingly twists the knife.

"I remember in high school you said you wanted to be an architect." Quickly, you search the crowd for someone else to talk to.

Now let's mentally rewind to the point where he asks, "What are you doing now?" What answer would you like to give? It could be that you have abandoned the goal from high school days for any number of very valid reasons. But there is still an answer that would give you great satisfaction in any situation, whether you're speaking to an old friend or someone you just met.

You probably know what that answer is. Again, go through that goal-setting process in Chapter 8. You may find that with a little analysis, your dream should remain just a dream, and that your present situation is more favorable than you thought. (In that case, begin looking ahead and setting goals on how to

> "It is only by risking our persons from one hour to another that we live at all. And often enough our faith beforehand in an uncertified result is the only thing that makes the result come true."
> — William James

improve that situation.) On the other hand, if your dream even begins to appear achievable, you'll have a plan to get started.

NEWFOUND ENERGY

With a plan, your expectations are raised. You can't help but feel better about your chances for success, because you'll be doing something you really care about. Those who have made this commitment notice a remarkable increase in their energy levels.

Marsha Sinetar, author of *Do What You Love, the Money Will Follow*, tells of a young man who left a lucrative but unsatisfying career in computing to go back to college and study psychology. Adjusting to the lower income was difficult at first, but his commitment led him to find part-time work to pay his tuition.

"Once upon a time I would have quit when the going got rough," Sinetar quotes the young man as saying. "But now I'm eager to do what I must to stick to my choice."

Earl Nightingale mentioned that newfound energy in *Lead the Field*: "Once a person fully understands that the goals that are important to him can become real in his life, well, it's like opening a jack-in-the-box: all sorts of interesting and exciting things begin to happen. Quite often, we become truly alive for the first time in our lives. We look back at our former lives and realize we were shuffling along in a kind of lockstep."

> "The amount of satisfaction you get from life depends largely on *your* own ingenuity, self-sufficiency, and resourcefulness. People who wait around for life to supply their satisfaction usually find boredom instead."
> — Dr. William Menninger, *Self-Understanding*

Maybe we shuffle along because that comes easiest, at least at first. Charles Garfield, author of *Peak Performers*, says we have more confidence in the brain's logical ability than in its imaginative ability. But in his research, peak performers were found to have highly developed faculties of logic and imagination.

If you're still not comfortable with the idea of imagining your success and then going on to achieve it, consider this: Every product or service ever used began as an idea! Someone thought it could be done, and then set about doing it.

At WYNCOM, we have produced a motivational videotape featuring goals that appear on the screen. These ambitious "stretch" goals refer to the growth we are planning for next year, the work atmosphere of WYNCOM ("WYNCOM is a fun-loving company"), and the continuation and enhancement of our strategic alliances with key business partners. We want all WYNCOM employees to focus on these goals and mentally see them being achieved.

The power of the self-fulfilling prophecy can be found in short-term situations as well. In preparing a teleconference on basketball instruction, a process that took several months, I had scheduled an appointment

> **"Vision is the art of seeing things invisible."**
> — Jonathan Swift

with UCLA basketball coach Jim Harrick to videotape an interview. I flew into Los Angeles the night before the appointment, which was set for 8 o'clock the next morning. At 3 a.m. our cameraman arrived with bad news. The airline had lost his camera. We didn't panic (at least not outwardly). "This is Los Angeles," I told the crew, reminding myself of that at the same time. "There *is* a television camera in Los Angeles." I could still see us completing our work as scheduled.

Our first idea was to call the night news desks at the local television stations. They couldn't spare their equipment, but did refer us to some local freelancers. At 5 a.m., I found one who agreed to shoot the interview three hours later.

In that situation, we were committed to the short-term goal of finding a camera and to the long term goal of complet-

> **"Make no little plans. They have no magic to stir men's blood. Make big plans: Aim high in hope and work."**
> — attributed to D.H. Burnham

ing work for the teleconference. We fully expected to succeed; our energy level was high, even though no one had had much sleep; we persisted in searching for what was needed; and we succeeded. Had we been in a more remote location, I am confident we would have succeeded there, too. We may have had to adjust our schedule or otherwise alter plans for the teleconference, but we would have used our considerable energy to come up with the best possible solution to keep our goal in sight.

Another example of the power of the self-fulfilling prophecy as a part of everyday business can be found in negotiating. The skills of negotiation, so vital to success in business, are subject to the attitudes of those involved. In *Everything's Negotiable . . . When You Know How to Play the Game,* authors Eric William Skopec and Laree S. Kiely say a positive attitude is essential to success in negotiations.

"Our nonverbal signals are almost always unintentional," they say. "But they are seldom ignored by the people with whom we deal. If we feel threatened, our behavior will signal fear or uncertainty, and the other party may rush in to take advantage. Similarly, if we are angry, our behavior will signal hostility, and other players will move to defend themselves. . . . If you approach negotiation with a positive attitude, your behavior will signal confidence, self-assurance and trustworthiness. Other people will warm to you and support your efforts to make the negotiation a positive, productive experience."

LEADING OTHERS WITH THE PYGMALION EFFECT

Good self-leadership can make you a much better leader of others. You can help those who work for you use the power of self-fulfilling prophecy by providing positive expectations of their work. This principle has been called the Pygmalion effect.

In Greek mythology, Pygmalion was a sculptor who created an ivory statue so beautiful that he fell in love with it. The goddess Aphrodite, seeing that the sculptor actually had come to believe his creation was real, breathed life into the statue. This myth became the basis for a George Bernard Shaw play called *Pygmalion*, which in turn inspired the Broadway musical *My Fair Lady*.

Business consultant Paul Loftus, writing about the Pygmalion factor in *Canadian Banker* magazine, says the way a task is presented to an employee can be crucial to the result. Simply saying, "This will be a tough job" could be misinterpreted as "I expect you to have problems with this one." For best results, Loftus says, give a positive message like this: "I know it's a tight deadline and you'll be pushed for time, but that's why I'm giving to you. I know you can do it. If you need assistance, please let me know.' The message I communicate is that I have full confidence in the person's ability to complete the task successfully and also that I am available in the event of a problem."

But there is more to the Pygmalion effect than simply positive words. For true effectiveness, these words must be accompanied by actions. As leaders, we need to provide those we lead with not only encouragement but also the *resources* to do the job. In other words, the self-fulfilling prophecy is something to be practiced actively, not passively. If the actions don't match the words, then all the positive talk can wind up being counterproductive.

> "Whether you think you can or think you can't . . . either way, you're right."
> — Henry Ford

There are a number of adjectives we could use to describe the leader who causes people to live up to high expectations. Among them: accessible, open-minded, instructive, sensitive, aware, positive, believing, trusting, confident, encouraging, bold, enterprising, adventuresome, innovative, accepting, patient, forgiving, creatively dissatisfied, demanding and appreciative.

Peter Drucker, in *The Effective Executive*, says: "The executive who focuses on contribution also stimulates others to develop themselves, whether they are subordinates, colleagues or superiors. . . . People in general, and knowledge workers in particular, grow according to the demands they make on themselves. They grow according to what they consider to be achievement and attainment. If they demand little of themselves, they will remain stunted. If they demand a good deal of themselves, they will grow to giant stature — without any more effort than is expended by the nonachievers."

The self-fulfilling prophecy takes logical steps to a conclusion, as it did in our efforts to find a video camera. Your choice of a worthy, satisfying goal is followed by higher expectations, which are followed by an increased energy level. More energy will provide you with persistence. Remember the Calvin Coolidge quote from Chapter 8: "Persistence and determination alone are omnipotent."

Many of us have the terrible habit of dismissing our own ideas for one reason only — they're ours! Groucho Marx got lots of laughs by saying he wouldn't want to belong to any club that would have him as a member. If you wouldn't want to act on an idea because you thought of it, then you're telling the same joke. Unfortunately, this one's on you.

You don't have to be a Thomas Edison to effectively use the power of your ideas. "Creative imagination is not something reserved for the poets, the philosophers, the inventors," writes Maxwell Maltz in *Psycho-cybernetics*. "It enters into our every act, for imagination sets the goal, the picture which our automatic mechanism works on. We act, or fail to act, not because of will as is so commonly believed, but because of imagination."

Now that you are well on your way to being an effective self-leader, you can use the ideas in this book to gain the power of self-fulfilling prophecy. You can set goals. You can conquer procrastination and other time-robbers. You can find time to think. You can think effectively. What you think is certainly up to you. But your thoughts will indeed shape your future.

WORDS FROM WYNCOM

"I am striving for excellence in what I do and try to add to my knowledge whenever I have an opportunity. I would endeavor to take those bits of wisdom provided by our speakers that I feel can help me to improve my life and review them often until they finally become second nature. Ideas such as 'live each day as if it were your last' and 'invest in others' emotional bank accounts' help me to be satisfied with my life and make each day satisfying."
— *Elaine Rutherford*

"The materials have helped me keep my values and intentions — like graduating from college — in line. But I can't imagine, even after I graduate, working for a more caring, giving and understanding company than WYNCOM." — *Ashley Begley*

"I feel that exposure to the best motivational materials on the market has truly impacted me, but I still have plenty of room to grow further. . . . The effect of the materials has been to instill in me that even the most insignificant suggestion or idea could be the beginning of the wave of the future." — *Anna Lee Ginter*

"Plan ahead, but get set to change the plan without notice. Life has a way of shaking the tree when the comfort level is high. WYNCOM'S influence on me has given me the strength to trust myself no matter what situation arises — both professionally and personally. I recently lost my best friend, my husband, and I know that the exposure to empowerment here greatly affected the manner in which I am dealing with my loss." — *Tyra Swilo*

"Who knows what my future holds? My plan is to live life to the fullest and take advantage of every opportunity that presents itself — physically and mentally. The times I've sat in on Dr. Waitley's, Peters' or Covey's sessions, I've picked up new knowledge of how to better myself, new ideas on managing my life." — *Terri Cecil*

"Working with the motivational materials WYNCOM promotes has affected both my professional and personal life. Dr. Waitley reaffirms my belief in self-efficacy. His programs lift my spirit and motivate me to have confidence in my actions. Dr. Peters reaffirms my belief in valuing differences. His take on hiring people other than those with impeccable resumes and those with life experiences and daring delights me. He reaffirms my belief that the energetic person willing to step out of the expected norm is a valued worker. Lyle Sussman and Sam Deep offer enhancements to problem-solving techniques, ways to reach confident decisions with greater ease. Ken Davis enhances my knowledge of the workings of people, what to value (the supporters), what to avoid (the underminers)." — *Carolyn Coffey*

"I have some goals that would cause a great deal of people to say, 'That guy is crazy.' I want to publish my own book one day. Watch out, WYNCOM! I may be your next motivational speaker!" — *Scott Via*

"Our motivational courses have helped me see things in my career life more from the perspective of 'the other guy.' It helps to be more tolerant of others' different viewpoints. Being less critical and listening to others helps to prevent a lot of problems — in the workplace and at home." — *Russ Lampe*

For further reading . . .

Covey, Stephen R. *The Seven Habits of Highly Effective People* (Simon & Schuster). Part One, "Paradigms and Principles," includes inspired discussions of the power of the Pygmalion effect and the self-fulfilling prophecy.

Daniels, Aubrey C. *Bringing Out the Best in People: How to Apply the Astonishing Power of Positive Reinforcement* (McGraw-Hill). This book is an enthusiastic but practical guide to applying the self-fulfilling prophecy principle as a manager and supervisor — leading others to their best performance by expecting the best from them and by reinforcing the best in them.

Deep, Sam, and Lyle Sussman. *What To Say To Get What You Want* (Addison Wesley). This book of specific words for "getting the best" begins with Deep and Sussman's first "commandment of change": "Expect the Best."

Deep, Sam, and Lyle Sussman. *Yes, You Can!* (Seminars by Sam Deep). Chapter 1, "Think Positively," includes a number of lists of specific, practical tips for expecting the best and fulfilling those expectations.

Douglas, Mack R. *How to Make a Habit of Succeeding* (Pelican). This book is built on the concept of the self-fulfilling prophecy, with its discussion of the "power of purpose," its assertion that "goals can change your life" and its advice to "build confidence and succeed."

Peters, Tom. *The Pursuit of WOW! Every Person's Guide to Topsy-Turvy Times* (Vintage). The section titled "Attaining Perpetual Adolescence," beginning on page 301, is an upbeat, even offbeat, guide to believing in possibilities.

Skopec, Eric William, and Laree S. Kiely. *Everything's Negotiable . . . When You Know How to Play the Game* (Amacom). This book is an excellent guide to negotiation, including a good discussion of the importance of expecting a favorable outcome.

Waitley, Denis. *Empires of the Mind: Lessons to Lead and Succeed in a Knowledge-Based World* (Morrow). Chapter 7, "Self-Leadership and Attitude: Your Self-Fulfilling Prophecy," is the best short introduction I know to the power of self-fulfilling prophecies, concluding with advice on how to "concentrate on the real thing."

Waitley, Denis. *Timing Is Everything: Turning Your Seasons of Success into Maximum Opportunities* (Nelson). Chapter 4, "The Season for Dreaming," is a powerful expansion of the concept "You must BEGIN your success with a dream."

ABOUT THE AUTHOR

Larry Holman is the guiding force behind the "Eleven Lessons in Self-Leadership" program featuring Stephen Covey, Tom Peters and Denis Waitley and moderated by Linda Ellerbee. Uplinked by satellite from San Diego and downlinked to 100 American cities on November 15, 1995, the program is a milestone in distance learning.

Holman, who holds an MBA from the University of Louisville, has taught management at the university level and served as executive director of the University of Kentucky Management Center during 1981-86. In 1986, Holman founded teleClinic, a company dedicated to using teleconference technology to provide long-distance learning. Five years later, teleClinic evolved into the Productivity Improvement Forum, Inc., which produced the international video teleconference "2001: Lessons in Leadership."

In 1992, Bunny and Larry Holman founded WYNCOM, Inc., a communications company engaged in the marketing and production of educational, professional development and management skills programs. As president and chairman respectively of WYNCOM, the Holmans have produced hundreds of live programs under the banner of the "Lessons in Leadership" distinguished speaker series, which is co-sponsored by selected colleges and universities throughout the United States and in Canada.